Fearless HR

Driving Business Results

David C. Forman

Sage Learning Systems Press
San Diego, California

Printed in the United States of America

Published by Sage Learning Systems Press.

San Diego, California

www.sagelearning.com

While the author has made every effort to represent third party information accurately, he is not responsible for information that may have been changed, updated or modified from its initial version.

For permissions and potential speaking engagements, please contact the author.

ISBN -13 9781514238004

ISBN-10 1514238004

To the Circle of Cousins ...

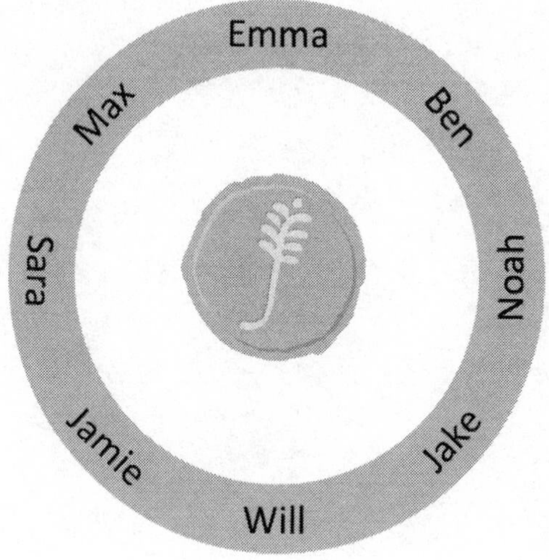

May you dream your dreams, live your dreams and help others achieve theirs.

g

Table of Contents

FOREWORD

What a delight to read and savor David Forman's new book *Fearless HR*. He has had a unique perch from which to observe the evolving HR profession, having worked inside leading companies, then working across many companies at HCI. He has a knack for recognizing key themes, explaining them clearly, then offering evidence to rebut and tools to replace traditional reputational challenges faced by HR.

One reason I resonate, appreciate, and like his work is that it focuses on what is right with HR more than what is wrong. Some prophets see what is wrong, tell the people they are damned and going to hell. Others see what is wrong and give them a pathway to heaven. David's work offers HR professionals a positive pathway forward, based on evidence and practical tools.

Let me share some of the themes in the HR world that are highlighted in this book and that will help HR professionals get on a pathway to a positive future.

First, HR is not about HR. In leading companies, HR shapes business value because HR does not start with HR, but with the business. The scorecard of good HR is the business scorecard. HR investments help deliver product innovation, geographic expansion, and customer intimacy growth strategies. David's primary message is to start HR with the business, not with HR. In our work, we want to go beyond strategic HR where business strategy is a mirror in which HR reflects business goals; strategy can be a window so that HR work is being connected to external customers and to investor confidence (called HR outside in). Customers are increasingly involved with staffing (sourcing and interviewing candidates), training (designing, attending, and teaching), performance management (doing 720 more than 360), and leadership (leadership brand). Investor confidence increases when they monitor quality of leadership through a leadership capital index assessing individual leaders and human capital systems. HR investments drive employee productivity and organization capabilities which deliver strategy which increase customer and investor share. David's views of Fearless HR reinforce this outside in perspective.

Second, HR is not just about talent. For 20 years HR has been focused on talent (called labor force, workforce, employees, staff, and people). The war for talent has been the dominant metaphor for HR. Leading organizations are now pivoting from a focus on war for talent to victory through organization. Individuals are champions, but teams win championships. Leading HR professionals manage both the workforce and workplace, talent and teamwork, individual competence and organization capabilities. Under the adage, culture eats strategy for breakfast, HR insights on culture move HR to a leading contributor to sustained business results. We increasingly see HR professionals being the architect for an organization's capabilities like: speed/agility/change, collaboration/teamwork, innovation, strategic unit, information, risk management, leadership depth, and talent, Auditing and delivering these capabilities become a marvelous next agenda for HR professionals. David's last chapter on mindset is an example of moving to a cultural shift within the HR profession. Instead of management by objectives, we pivot to management by mindset, or shared culture.

Third, HR for HR has arrived. HR professionals need to apply their insights to their own function and work. Innovative HR practices have facilitated business results by focusing less on bureaucratic processes and more on simple and integrated solutions. Complex performance appraisals are replaced with informed conversations which ensure accountability. Training programs are not bounded by attendance within a prescribed course, but a process before, during, and after the course. Technology enabled hiring, training, and compensation help deliver the administrative work of HR so that more attention can be focused on strategic HR. HR departments are increasingly becoming professional services units within their organizations where they turn their expertise (on people, performance, information, and work) into line manager client value. As David so eloquently demonstrates, HR analytics have helped make HR investments that have business impact. One of the most useful messages of this book is that it builds on the past to create a future. Some HR books make bold statements about the future and don't appreciate the vast amount of HR insights that has been established.

Fourth, HR professionals don't just have competencies, they demonstrate competencies that deliver business results. After decades of research, we have a very thorough sense of the competencies for HR professionals. We have synthesized this competency work into the "HR food groups" where there are domains of what HR professionals should know and do. These domains include

1. Strategic positioner. HR professionals have to know how to position their business for future success.

2. Credible activist. HR professionals have to build personal relationships of trust to help organizations turn strategy into personal action.

3. Capability builder. HR professional shave to create cultures or capabilities that enable the organization as a whole to be stronger than individual competencies.

4. Innovative and integrated HR work. HR professionals must move beyond isolated HR practices to integrated HR solutions. These solutions means that HR activities in staffing, succession, training, compensation, organization design, communication, and so forth need to be connected to solve business problems.

5. Information and analytics. HR professionals have to come to business discussions with data that informs business decisions. Evidence based HR should inform choices.

Between the "strategy" (where the business is headed) and the "individual" (through credible activist), HR professionals manage flows of capability, human capital systems, information to bridge future direction and present actions.

We have found that when HR professionals demonstrate these competencies, not only are they seen as more effective HR professionals, but business performance goes up.

So, how do my themes connect to this remarkable book? They clearly overlap. David's book and my themes do not overlap 100% which is wonderful because it opens the field for positive exploration. Again, what I like most about this book is the focus on what is right more than what is wrong with HR. Rather than lament the inevitable challenges to innovative HR, I hope we can appreciate the pathway to a better future.

Dave Ulrich
Rensis Likert Professor of Business
University of Michigan
Partner, The RBL Group

INTRODUCTION

The spotlight is squarely on the HR profession today, and this focus presents both great challenges and opportunities. The spotlight shines brightly because leaders realize that companies don't create value, people do. It continues to shine because most of the market valuation of a company is based on intangible assets, not tangible ones. People are the drivers of intangible assets. And the HR profession is under greater scrutiny now because it is the single function in an organization that touches every employee.

The challenges that arise from being *"center stage"* are that HR has not yet found its own identity and purpose. It has been the subject of articles that want to *"blow up HR"* because it is ineffective. It has endeavored to escape its administrative past, but with mixed results. Like any overhead function, HR has sought greater recognition and credibility, but this has not always been gained. Even leading HR executives acknowledge that *"HR is not the most admired profession."* And there are historical perceptions of HR, rooted in the past century, that continue to haunt the profession today.

Fearless HR is about HR's purpose and identity going forward. It is about *driving business results.* It is about improving the competitive position of the company and its bottom line. It is about being a business leader, not a department head or a passive participant at a table full of unequals. It is about leveraging the talent of an organization to improve performance and productivity. And it is about being fearless, bold and willing to take risks for the business to be successful.

Key Topics

There are two parts to *Fearless HR*. Part One focuses on the past so that HR can move forward. Over the years, people have developed various perceptions about HR. We all know these perceptions exist but fail to address them because it might be awkward or uncomfortable. The problem is that these beliefs become even more engrained in corporate memory if they are allowed to persist. Mindsets are powerful and difficult to change, but the first step has to be acknowledging these perceptions and then examining the evidence to determine their relevance today. Five historical perceptions about HR are addressed in Part One.

Part Two focuses on the opportunities for HR moving forward. But before these opportunities can be realized, there are serious issues that must be addressed. HR, for example, needs to be as fast and as nimble as the business itself. *Fearless HR* identifies four steps HR must take to *drive business results*: 1) its talent and capabilities must be better, 2) its professional networks must be broader, more inclusive and stronger, 3) the levers at its disposal must be used to both save costs and improve productivity, and 4) its mindset must be bolder. It is also important that these improvements occur in the right sequence. A fearless attitude, without HR being able to deliver the goods, is misplaced and can lead to arrogance as opposed to enhanced professional confidence.

The double-helix visual below depicts the specific topics in Parts One and Two, and shows the three business results that are the emphasis of the new HR.

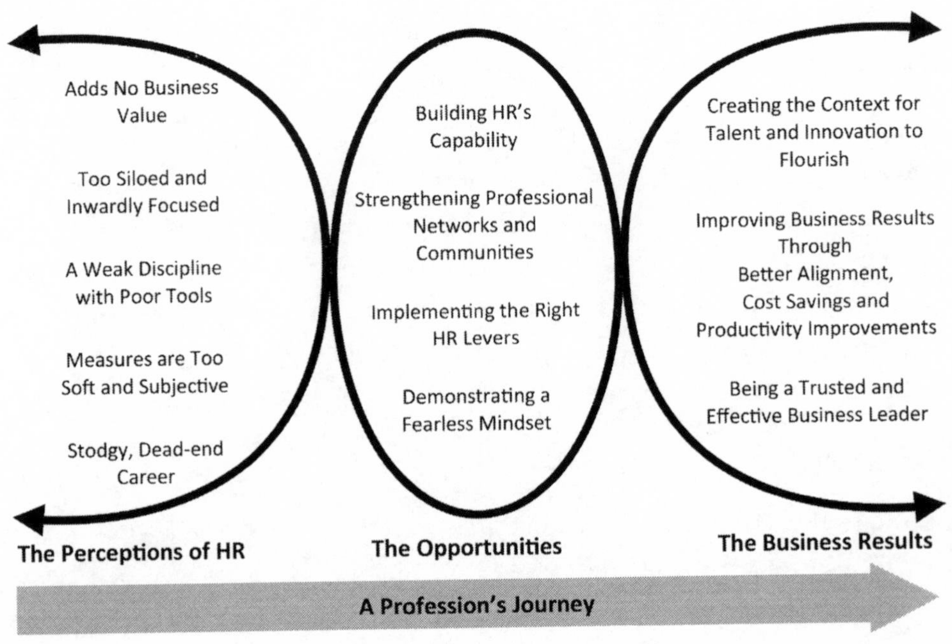

There are several themes that appear throughout *Fearless HR*. These themes have roots in my own background, first as a business leader in the training industry and then as the Chief Learning Officer for The Human Capital Institute (HCI) for more than a decade. I also see these themes as helping to distinguish *Fearless HR* from other HR books and articles. One key differentiator—identifying and addressing five perceptions of HR that have been held over the years--has already been highlighted. The other distinctive themes are:

- **Business Focus.** This is a business book about HR, not an HR book about business. HR professionals must develop stronger business acumen, focus on strategy first, and be comfortable with facts, figures, financial statements and the language of the business.. My background is in the training business, from instructional designer to consultant to learning system integrator and eventually to president of a $40 million company. I have always viewed HR through the lens of the business.

- **Strategic HR.** Most of *Fearless HR* focuses on strategic as opposed to operational HR activities. The operational aspects (i.e., benefits administration, compensation, personnel policies) are important to employees and must function smoothly, but the greatest benefits come from more strategic practices such as improving the workforce and workplace and employing HR Levers to drive business results. The HR Capability Framework (HRCF) presented in Part Two is mainly strategic in orientation as is the volume of best practices and research that is discussed.

- **Evidence-based Decision-making.** HR professionals are accused of being good with words, but not numbers. This view, just like the five historical perceptions in Part One, is an oversimplification and increasingly not true. The truth is that HR is a data-rich environment. It includes, for example, more than 25 years of research on how HR practices impact business results. New human capital analytics are being reported monthly, if not more frequently, by leading organizations. HR can be just as data-driven as finance and operational functions if this research is utilized and embraced.

- **Synthesizing Research and Thought Leadership.** There are many thought-leaders, authors and researchers who have influenced the HR profession over the years. Among the many that I draw from frequently are Dave Ulrich, Dan Pink, Gary Hamel, John Boudreau, Jim Collins, Marcus Buckingham, Ram Charan, and John Kotter. I have endeavored to synthesize their excellent work in one place that is easily accessible. I have learned from my decade teaching HCI's classes that participants really appreciate getting to know the work of the leading experts in our field. It is enjoyable to attach names and faces to facts and figures. There are over 150 references in the *Fearless HR* list of books and articles.

- **Practical Approach.** The overarching theme of *Fearless HR* is that HR can and should drive business results. This theme provides clarity to HR's purpose and identity. While many people now agree with this future vision, they are unsure *"what to do next."* *Fearless HR* includes a number of practical tools and templates that can be applied in different settings. In fact, over 45 actionable tools are presented across the nine chapters. I know from my experiences with thousands of HR professionals in classes and conferences that these tools make a difference and enable change to occur more easily.

A Final Word

I will say more about all the people who have contributed to *Fearless HR* in the Acknowledgements at the end of the book. There are so many people to thank for their support, insight and wisdom. This is just an advanced shout out to colleagues and family.

HR is a profession at a flash point. It can move forward, make enduring contributions, drive results and be fearless. Or HR can be shackled by past perceptions, uncertain of its role and questioning its own efficacy. Choices are being made every day, and it is encouraging to see HR driving business results in companies such as Google, Boeing, SAS, FedEx, and numerous small and medium-sized businesses. The future is being played out right in front of us. But before professions and organizations can transform, people must transition. *Fearless HR* is for each HR professional as he or she contemplates the next steps to take.

At the end of the day, I am a teacher, curious questioner and storyteller. In the work I have done with SHRM and more extensively with HCI, I have listened and learned from the best. I hope the collected knowledge, research and messages of *Fearless HR* are digestible and useful. I hope that the tools and templates lead to actions and changes. I hope that the stories are both engaging and thought provoking. The final test, of course, will be the extent to which *Fearless HR* makes an impact on you and your professional career. I hope it does.

Part 1

The Perceptions of HR

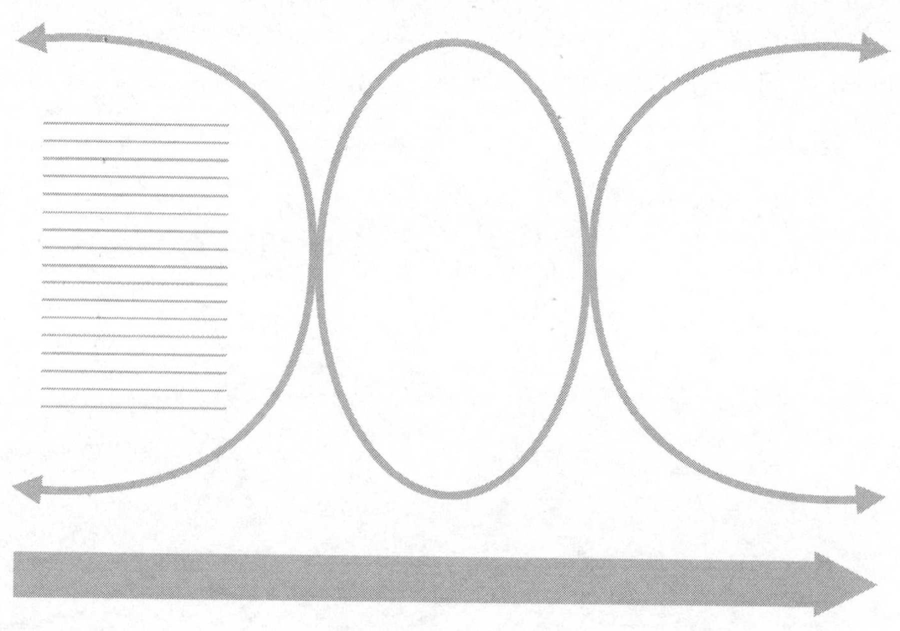

The profession of HR must confront its past before it can take advantage of new opportunities to make more lasting and significant contributions. This juxtaposition is not unique to HR. The philosopher George Santayana famously said: *"Those who cannot remember the past are condemned to repeat it."* While HR is a relatively new profession—slightly more than a century old—it has attracted its share of detractors. It is not a well-kept secret that negative perceptions of HR exist. Unfortunately, many of these beliefs go unchallenged, and therefore become even more entrenched. These perceptions remain today and influence how HR is perceived and valued.

It is also true that today there is a great deal of data and research pertaining to HR practices and their efficiency, effectiveness and impact. It should be possible, therefore, to examine these historical perceptions in light of the research findings. Are these perceptions accurate? Do the data corroborate or refute these beliefs? Is there another reality that needs to be aired?

Fearless HR presents five historical perceptions of HR. Even though each perception is treated in a separate chapter, they interact and affect each other. For example, if a person subscribes to the belief that HR does not add value to the business, they probably also believe that HR's tools and measures are weak. The five perceptions of HR are highlighted below.

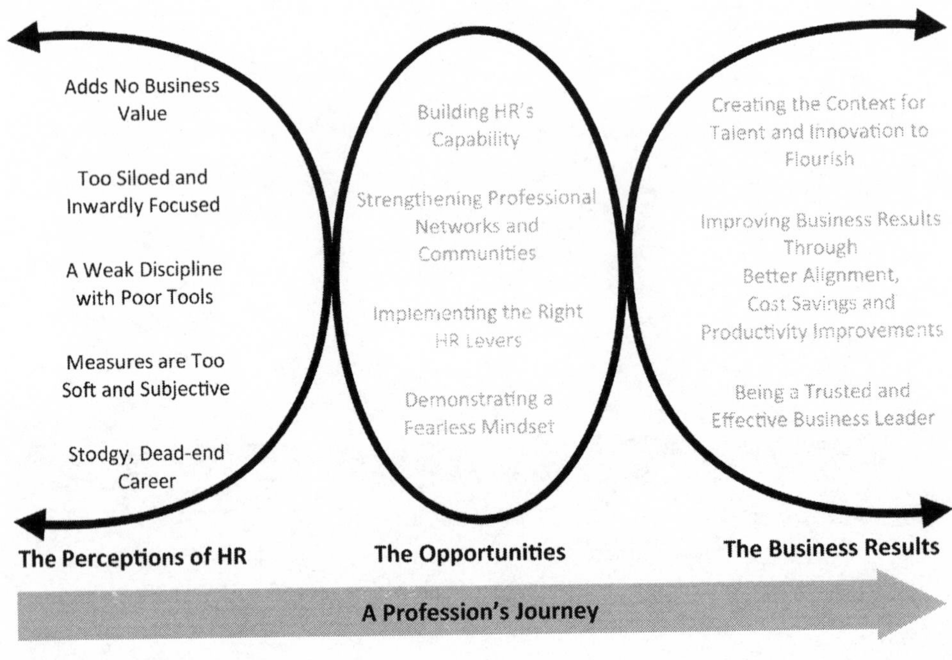

The organizational structure for each of the five chapters in Part One is identical. There is a brief overview that describes the perception, its historical relevance and reason for existence. Then, the following information is presented:

- **The Evidence:** This treatment synthesizes the research, best practices and thought leadership that pertain to that specific perception. While this synthesis is not exhaustive (there are other studies that could be included), it is detailed and specific. Usually this section is eight to twelve pages in length.

- **Recommendations and Insights.** Four recommendations and insights are presented based on the evidence previously cited. These recommendations are *my observations*; you may take other insights from the research as well. The hardest part in developing this discussion is limiting the recommendations to the manageable number of four. There are many possible interpretations of the data, but it is important to prioritize the most relevant insights so that actions can be taken.

- **Tools and Templates.** Five to six practical tools are presented for each perception. These tools are related to the best practices and research presented in the chapter, and their purpose is to aid in implementing key findings and recommendations.

With this structure in mind, let's first consider probably the most pervasive and far-reaching perception of all: HR Does Not Add Value to the Business. This perception is particularly troublesome because it directly conflicts with HR's future to drive business results as espoused in *Fearless HR*. Let's see what the evidence says.

Chapter 1

Perception One:
HR Does Not Add Value to the Business

> *"HR wants to add value, to contribute in meaningful ways to employees and line managers inside the company and to customers, communities, partners and investors outside the company. At times, those on the journey have been the target of snipers who discount HR's value and want to send it back to its administrative beginnings. At other times, progress has been slowed by cynics who doubt that HR can overcome its legacy and fully contribute."*
>
> *Dave Ulrich, 2008*

There are at least two contributing factors to the belief that HR adds little or no value to an organization. First, HR does have a strong administrative past. The antecedent of the Society for Human Resource Management (SHRM) in 1948 was the American Society of Personnel Administration.

- Harbors a deep conviction that better talent (human capital) leads to better corporate performance.
- Spends at least 20% of their time in talent reviews and practices; in many leading companies, this percentage grew to 30 to 40%.
- Establishes a gold standard for talent that is clearly articulated throughout the organization so that second-rate talent would not be hired or retained.
- Takes direct responsibility for building talent pools and succession planning for leadership and strategic positions.
- Holds all managers accountable for strengthening talent pools and creating environments in which talent can flourish.
- Teaches other leaders.

The War for Talent was hugely significant in the first decade of the Twenty-first Century, largely because of McKinsey's reputation and sway with major business leaders. The Talent Mindset findings did not come from an HR industry association or a boutique consulting firm; they came from the preeminent strategic consulting organization in the world. Many CEOs took notice and began to change their behavior because of the prestige of McKinsey and its impact particularly among members of Boards of Directors

Comparing Industry Peers

A number of research studies were completed in the first decade of the 21st Century that compared the practices of high performing organizations to their less distinguished industry peers. As discussed, this research does not prove that talent practices cause high performance; but it may show that a relationship exists. And when a number of studies show the same correlation again and again, it can lend credence to the finding that talent matters to organizational performance. A selective sample of these comparative research studies follow with the more recent studies being presented last.

1. *"The Human Capital Edge"* by Bruce Pfau and Ira Kay in 2002. These researchers from Watson Wyatt (at that time) used three different studies to examine the impact of specific talent practices on financial performance. Over 750 companies were examined in their Human Capital Index research and the results were clear and compelling: over a five year period, companies with a low human capital index yielded a 21% return for shareholders while companies with a high rating returned 64% to shareholders. Their Work USA research also clearly establishes a direct link between employee satisfaction and shareholder returns. They present data to demonstrate that leaders and companies with a strong talent mindset outperform those that do not by a factor of 2 to1.

One of the unique aspects of their research is the delineation of specific talent practices that have the most impact on market value during the time period studied (1996-2001). The five practice areas showing the biggest impact are:

Talent Practice Areas	Impact on Market Value
Recruiting and Retention Excellence	7.8%
Total Rewards and Accountability	16.5%
Collegial, Flexible Workplace	9.0%
Communications Integrity	7.1%
Focused HR Service Technologies	6.5%

Figure 1-1: Impact of Talent Practices on Market Value

2. Research reported by Sears in Successful Talent Strategies (2003). Sears reports research conducted by Towers-Perrin (at the time) that shows five key talent practices that separate successful from unsuccessful companies. These talent practices are:

1. Attract and retain people with skills to succeed
2. Engage and increase employee commitment
3. Align human resource programs with strategy
4. Communicate across the organization
5. Train and develop the workforce effectively

Their research showed that the most difficult talent practice to accomplish and sustain is *"engage and increase employee commitment."* This finding is a precursor to the engagement studies that would follow over the next decade.

3. *"Good to Great"* by Jim Collins in 2001. In the biggest selling business book of all time, Jim Collins adds insights to the practice of talent management. He makes the key point that *companies making the good to great transition* don't first set strategy and mission, they *"get the right people on the bus, the wrong people off the bus and the right people in the right seats—and then they figure out* *where to drive it."* He goes on to emphasize that the old adage that *people are your most important asset* is wrong. The ***right people*** are.

The Collins research, just like the McKinsey analysis before it, had a profound impact on business unit leaders and executives. The *"Good to Great"* research was not only credible, it set a new standard. The language that Collins and his team used began to appear in corporate boardrooms. The 6Rs and *"the bus"* became popular metaphors for what leaders should be asking: do we have the right people, in the right job, with the right skills, at the right place in the right time for the right cost (i. e., the 6Rs)?

4. High Performance Work Systems (HPWS) research by Brian Becker and Mark Huselid as reported in *"The HR Scorecard"* in 2001. This research creates a Human Capital Index and then compares the bottom and top 10% of organizations on HR and business performance. The differences between these two groups are significant.

- The top 10% of organizations devote more resources, time and focus to recruiting, training, team collaboration, aligning performance and recognition.
- The top tier organizations are much more likely to have developed a clear vision and communicated it effectively to all employees.
- In terms of outcomes, the top 10% Human Capital Index organizations had half the turnover, four times sales per employee and more than three times market to book value (which is an indicator of the extent to which management has increased shareholder value).

5. *"Integrated Talent Management"* by the IBM Institute for Business Value and HCI, 2008. This three-part study examines a variety of factors but first focuses on the question of the impact of talent practices. Their findings from a survey of 1000 organizations are:

"Overall, investment in talent management makes a difference. Our study highlights that both smaller and larger companies that invest in talent management practices are more likely to outperform their industry peers. Further, high performing companies are more likely ***to act on*** *data and make improvements."*

Companies that have taken further steps to ***integrate talent practices***—and not just have separate talent initiatives—are even more successful vis a vis their competitors. This study is significant because it is one of the first to emphasize an integrated system as opposed to a collection of distinct talent practices.

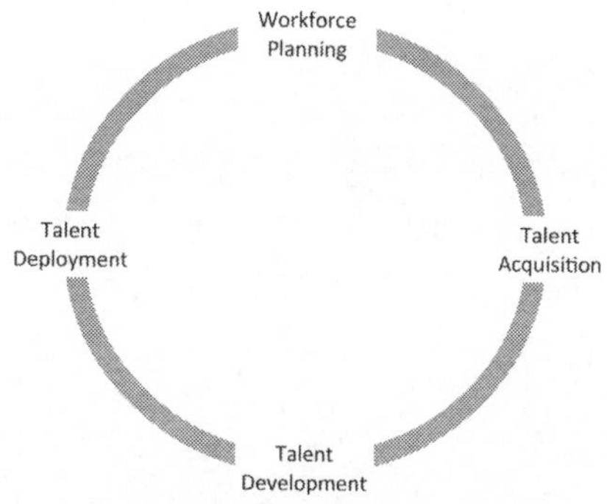

Figure 1-2: An Integrated Talent System

The four recommendations from this study to further integrate talent practices are:

- Develop a workforce analytics capability
- Embed collaboration and expertise location capabilities into existing work practices
- Incorporate talent marketplaces as a platform to more effectively deploy the workforce
- Rethink the role of employee development

6. *"Creating the Best Workplace on Earth"* by Rob Goffee and Gareth Jones in the Harvard Business Review, May, 2013. This qualitative study identifies companies that exhibit the qualities of an ideal organization.

"In a nutshell, it is a company where individual differences are nurtured; information is not suppressed or spun; the company adds value to the employees, rather than merely extracting it from them; the organization stands for something meaningful; the work itself is intrinsically rewarding; and there are no stupid rules."

Their dream company diagnostic is built around simple statements that may be common sense but are certainly not common practice.

- Let me be myself
- Tell me what's really going on
- Discover and magnify my strengths
- Make me proud I work here
- Make my work meaningful
- Don't hinder me with stupid rules

While this study does not link these characteristics to company performance or financial results as the others do, the findings are very similar to those from engagement and Best Places to Work research presented later in this chapter. These characteristics create an environment and context within which talent can flourish.

These six comparative studies—which represent different time periods and approaches—are only a small fraction of the studies that show a strong link among effective talent practices, employee attitudes and improved financial and business performance.

The Shift to Intangible Value

Baruch Lev first brought the concept of *Intangible Value* to the attention of the HR and talent communities when he postulated that for every $6 in market value of an organization only $1 is recorded on the balance sheet. The balance sheet records tangible assets such as equipment, facilities, technology and resources, but not the type of assets that are people-related and drive such outcomes as innovation, agility and responsiveness. This finding is of substantial interest to the HR community because intangible assets are largely nurtured, developed and leveraged through HR practices and actions.

Key Intangible Assets	
Execution of Corporate Strategy	Brand
Quality of Strategy	Quality of Customers and Partners
Management Credibility	Depth of Talent Pools
Ability to Innovate and Research Leadership	Engagement of the Workforce
Ability to Attract and Retain Talented Employees	Market Share

Figure 1-3: Intangible Assets

The importance of tangible versus intangible assets varies by industry and has shifted over time. In resource and process intensive industries such as manufacturing, oil exploration and mining, tangible assets still predominate. But increasingly today companies need to be resilient, innovative, global and flexible; and these are intangible, people-centric qualities.

One of the first public indications that market valuation was significantly changing was the 1995 IBM acquisition of Lotus, the Massachusetts-based software company. Lotus was the originator of the Lotus 123 spreadsheet and Lotus Notes collaborative tools. IBM paid $3.5 billion for Lotus, and this price made little sense based on traditional valuation methods for tangible assets. But IBM, just like Facebook and other technology companies today, said it was acquiring the people and their talent to develop future products, not buildings and materials. This practice has come to be called *acquihiring.*

The actual equation for the market shift from tangible to intangible asset valuation has been subject to debate. Ulrich and Smallwood (2003), report the following findings from the Brookings Institute and Baruch Lev.

Year	Intangible %	Tangible %
1982	38%	62%
1992	62%	38%
2000	85%	15%

Figure 1-4: Percentage of Market Valuation Provided by Tangible and Intangible Assets

Today, most people would suggest that intangibles account for 50 to 65% of a company's market valuation. The 85% figure is probably a vestige of inflated valuation from the Internet hysteria era; and while it may be true for some high tech startups even today, a more balanced picture obtains now. But focusing on the percentage differences between the two misses the point; the intangible number is still very large and it is malleable, controllable and can be improved.

The relationship between tangible and intangible assets is not an esoteric financial discussion. It is well understood by financial investors and Boards of Directors alike. There is an increasing recognition that the soft stuff (Intangibles) is actually the hard stuff that creates value. Ulrich and Smallwood (2003) discuss this shift in their book *"Why the Bottom Line Isn't."*

Members of Boards of Directors, who are charged with improving shareholder value and to whom CEOs report, are asking for data on the strength of talent practices and intangible assets. They clearly see the link between these practices and market valuation. HCI's corporate members report that talent metrics are regular entries on Board agendas, and the top three requested measures are 1) strength and depth of leadership talent pools, 2) employee engagement scores and actions, and 3) turnover within key talent segments. Because of the proven importance of intangible assets, an argument can be made that any Board of Directors that is NOT concentrating on intangibles is neglecting its responsibilities.

Comparing Talent Practices to Stock Value

There is a line of research that examines talent practices of organizations and their relationship to stock price over time. This research uses stock price as the ultimate outcome for a publically traded company, and while there may be a number of other factors that impact stock price, the quality of human capital practices is significant as we have seen in the discussion of intangibles. There are two noteworthy examples of this line of inquiry.

The first is the research done by Lauri Bassi and her colleagues (2011). In addition to being excellent researchers, Lauri Bassi and Dan McMurrer are licensed investment advisors who have created portfolios based on human capital practices. Their two oldest portfolios are based on the simple proposition that those organizations that invest more in educating, developing and training their employees will perform better than organizations in general. They have subsequently developed portfolios that focus on other aspects of human capital such as analytics and performance measures, and all of the portfolios have outperformed the S&P 500, with annualized performance gains from 3.4% to 14.0%. What is unique about this research is that the authors are literally putting their own money on the line.

With the publication of *"Good Company: Business Success in the Worthiness Era,"* Bassi extends her portfolios to address organizations that are socially conscious, transparent, reciprocal, collaborative and risk-takers. Using a *"Good Company Index,"* the results are similar to their earlier work: Companies with higher Good Company Index scores did better in the stock market over the last year, the last three years and the last five years than their industry match.

The second example of relating talent practices to stock price is from The Great Places to Work Institute (GPWI). For almost 30 years, the Institute has compiled the Fortune Best Places to Work lists that are published at the start of each year. This list is derived from the early work of Robert Levering that great places to work were about relationships and had three qualities: trust the people you work for; have pride in what you do and enjoy the people you work with. Later these themes were broadened into their current framework.

Dimension	Examples
Credibility	Communications are open and accessible Integrity in carrying out vision with consistency
Respect	Support professional development Collaborate with employees in relevant decisions Care for employees as individuals
Fairness	Equity—balanced treatment for all in terms of rewards Impartiality Justice
Pride	In personal job In work by the team or group In the organization's products and standing in the community
Camaraderie	Ability to be oneself Welcoming atmosphere Sense of family or team

Figure 1-5: The Great Places to Work Criteria

Using two indices—the Trust Index and the Culture Audit—GPWI surveys over 2 million people each year. When the Fortune 100 Best compares are compared to the S&P 500 and the Russell 3000, the results are that the Fortune Best companies have:

- About half the turnover
- Significantly more job applications
- Lower absenteeism
- Two to three times greater annualized returns from 1998 to 2009

As Jim Goodnight, CEO of SAS which is a company that is always on the Fortune 100 Best list, says, *"It turns out that doing the right thing, treating people right, is also the right thing for the company."*

The Human Capital Value Chain: Employees, Customers, Revenues

This research uses an explicit model to show the relationship among employee satisfaction, customer loyalty and business outcomes. An early example is the work done at Sears in the mid-1990s. This framework, known as the *"3 compellings,"* said that before Sears can be a compelling place for investors, it must be a compelling place to shop; and the key to a successful shopping experience is that Sears must be a compelling place to work. The data supported this linkage: a 5% increase in employee commitment led to a 1.8% increase in customer commitment and a .5% increase in financial results.

James Heskitt and colleagues have investigated the *"service profit chain"* for decades. His work on the Value Profit Chain (2003) and Ownership Quotient (2008) shows that the best predictor of greater financial results is customer loyalty. Customer loyalty is the extent to which a customer buys from the same company again and again. But the story does not stop with customer loyalty as the authors explain:

> *"Profit and growth are stimulated primarily by customer loyalty. Loyalty is a direct result of customer satisfaction. Satisfaction is largely influenced by the value of services provided to customers. Value is created by satisfied, loyal and productive employees. Employee satisfaction, in turn, results primarily from high-quality support services and policies that enable employees to deliver results to customers."*
>
> *James Heskitt*

This storyline is corroborated with data and further analysis, such as:

- Reichheld and Sasser estimate that a 5% increase in customer loyalty can produce profit increases from 25% to 85%.
- An insurance company study revealed that when key service workers leave the company, customer satisfaction dropped from 75% to 55%.

- Taco Bell discovered that the 20% of stores with the lowest turnover rates enjoyed double the sales and 55% higher profits than stores in the bottom 20%.
- FedEx has determined that a 1% increase in customer loyalty equates to $100 million in incremental revenue.

The Human Capital Institute (HCI) extended the profit value chain framework to create the Human Capital Value Chain. It is a visual model that depicts how leading companies today need to be successful in the workplace before succeeding in the marketplace. In the past companies may have set financial targets and emphasized treating customers with respect, but employees were not deemed to be as important. These organizations emphasized the right side of the Human Capital Value Chain. Today, successful companies start at the left side and follow through for strong financial performance.

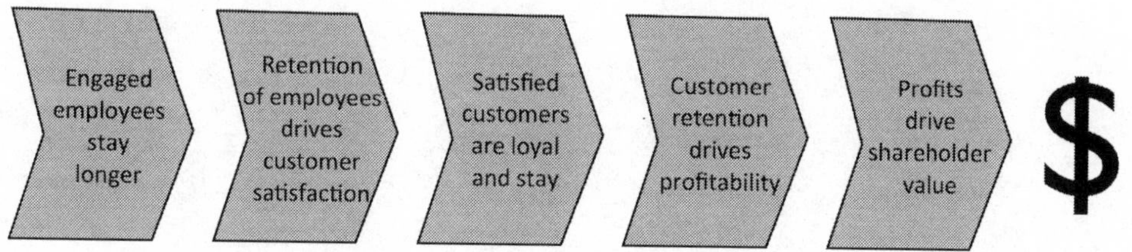

Figure 1-6: The Human Capital Value Chain

> *"You have to treat your employees like customers. When you treat them right, they will treat your outside customer right. This has been a powerful competitive weapon for us."*
>
> *Herb Kelleher, Retired*
> *CEO, Southwest Airlines*

Employee Engagement Research

Perhaps the longest continuing line of research linking workplace variables to outcomes is the study of engagement, first reported by the Gallup Corporation with its groundbreaking *"First Break All the Rules"* by Coffman and Buckingham (1998). While there are similarities among the concepts of employee satisfaction, happiness and engagement, the distinguishing factor of engagement is a behavioral component. An engaged employee believes in what they do, feels valued for it and is willing *to spend discretionary effort* to make the organization successful. As James Harter, Chief Scientist at Gallup has said: *"It is really the attitudes that predict if people are likely to show up to work, be highly productive, innovative and profitable."* (Talent Management, 2014)

A multi-million dollar engagement consulting industry grew from Gallup's early work, primarily because the data were compelling and demonstrated business impact. Engagement has been proven to be a leading indicator of turnover and productivity. Among key findings from a variety of consulting organizations:

- Actively disengaged employees are not only a negative influence; they cost the organization in lost productivity. Gallup estimates that the productivity decline for each actively disengaged employee can be calculated as $3400 for every $10,000 in fully combined salary and benefits (Gallup, 2002). So, for example, an actively disengaged person who makes $80,000 in salary and benefits costs the organization $27,200 in lost productivity.

- Up to 10% of an organization's performance can be attributed to employee engagement (Kenexa, 2011)

- Higher engagement leads to 31% increase in productivity, 37% higher sales and 3X greater innovation (TalentKeepeers, 2013)

- Best Buy knows that a .1% increase in engagement relates to $100,000 in incremental revenue at the store level.

In a 2013 Gallup survey, only 30% of the North American workforce is engaged, with 18% being actively disengaged, and a big collection of 50% who currently could go either direction. These percentages have stayed fairly consistent over the years, and some economists believe that poor engagement is costing the US economy $500 billion dollars annually. Gallup's report on the state of the American Workforce (2013) also serves to underscore the benefits of an engaged, committed workforce. It compared companies in the top and bottom quartile on engagement. The top quartile companies demonstrated important differences.

- 48% fewer safety accidents
- 37% lower absenteeism
- 28% less shrinkage (theft)
- 41% fewer quality incidents
- 10% higher customer metrics
- 21% higher productivity
- 22% higher profitability
- 65% lower turnover

While engagement findings have been discussed for several decades, and several thought leaders have called for expanding the concept to include enablement, alignment and readiness; engagement continues to be a significant workforce issue. Bersin (2015) cites engagement as a front-burner issue and potential significant business risk.

> *"If you think about it logically, engagement is all a company really has. We can build great leadership, hire top people, train people well and coach them expertly —but, if they do not like their jobs and the mission of the organization, then they will not deliver with quality."*
>
> *Josh Bersin, 2015*

These, then, are highlights from research that addresses the perception that HR does not add value to the organization. This is perhaps the most fundamental, serious and long-held perception of all. If HR truly does not add any value, then what is the point: Minimize the cost, outsource it and employ more technology. But this is not what the research findings show. While these studies employ different methods, there is a remarkable consistency of findings.

RECOMMENDATIONS AND INSIGHTS:

Each chapter in *Fearless HR* will have three to five recommendations/observations for you to consider. The following observations are based on the evidence presented and the myriad conversations I have had over the past fifteen years with students and colleagues.

1. **HR Does Impact the Business: Improving the Workplace and Workforce Makes a Difference.**

   As the synthesis of research in this chapter has shown, and as respected leaders like Jim Goodnight of SAS have said, businesses prosper when workplaces are improved. The goal is to create an environment and context within which talent can flourish, innovation can be fostered and employee potential is turned into performance. Study after study, time after time, research findings show a linkage among employee attitudes, talent practices and improved outcomes. There are still leaders who believe otherwise, but most leaders today, unlike a decade ago, either believe that talent practices matter or are willing to listen to a compelling argument. It is up to HR professionals to be able to assemble the research that HR makes a difference and make compelling business cases to influence leaders and managers who may not initially believe that these investments will be beneficial.

2. **The Real Big Deal for CEOs is Intangibles**

   Of all of the research evidence about the impact of talent practices, the one that has had the biggest impact on executives is the rise in the value of intangibles. It is not that the other research is not meaningful and compelling, because it is, especially from eminently credible sources such as McKinsey and Jim Collins. But CEOs, just like all of us, have bosses and constituencies they need to address. Two of these relationships are with Boards of Directors and the financial community, both of whom are very interested in intangibles.

Boards of Directors are charged with increasing shareholder value; and if a sizable percentage of this value is determined by intangible assets, then Boards want to monitor progress and trumpet improvements. Boards increasingly want CEOs and executive leaders to improve the intangibles scorecard and performance. Similarly, the financial community knows the role that intangibles play in market valuation, and they are also emphasizing the need for more visibility, tracking and improvements before recommending the company as a sound investment.

These priorities from both Boards and the financial community have moved CEOs to expand their perspectives, recognize that people-driven outcomes are vital to competitive positioning, and understand that before you can be successful in the marketplace, you first have to be successful in the workplace. HR professionals should know the intangible assets that are most important to their company, and incorporate them into their own agenda and action plans.

3. Mindsets Matter

There are two mindsets that pertain to the perception that *"HR adds no value"*. The first is the Talent Mindset of leaders as described by McKinsey in the *"War for Talent."* If leaders see employees as simply a cost to be controlled and do not recognize that they are also an asset to be leveraged; then progress will be difficult to achieve. If this situation exists, HR professionals have several fundamental choices to make

- Seek out leaders to work with who share a talent mindset, even if they exist at lower levels of the organization. Try to pick your battles.
- While mindsets dictate subsequent behavior, mindsets can be changed if leaders are willing to consider evidence. If reluctant leaders are open to this possibility, then consider a campaign to change their mindset. Build a compelling case for change that addresses both the rational and emotional aspects of change. Data alone will not be enough (Heath and Heath, 2010).

- The good news is that most executives and leaders today have been swayed by the research and other CEOs talent mindsets.
- If all else fails and your CEO is hierarchical and recalcitrant, find another opportunity.

4. The Leverage Point: Managers

It was Coffman and Buckingham (1997) who first verbalized what many had suspected: *people join companies but leave managers.* Research has proved this time and time again. A poor manager is always one of the top three or four reasons for unwanted turnover in organizations. Gallup later identified the drivers of engagement and 70% of them involve the employee's first line manager. Most other research organizations would agree, although the Corporate Executive Board (CEB) puts more of the emphasis on leaders; but it is clear that managers directly impact engagement and retention.

Good managers create a cycle of value—because of all the employees they impact based on span of control—and bad managers create a cycle of waste. John Sullivan has estimated that at least 40% of managers are in the latter category, and HCI has suggested that only 1 in 12 managers is intuitively good at improving engagement among their employees. The fact is that managers are rarely trained on engagement skills when newly promoted to the manager level.

Thoughtful companies have taken proactive steps to improve the *"employee-manager relationship."* Among the actions that have been successful are:

- Provide a variety of ways to be promoted beyond becoming a manager. If the only way to be promoted is to become a manager, bad things can happen. At Facebook, only people wanting to be people managers are given this opportunity.
- Recognize that you engage one good employee at a time. Broad solutions don't work; it has to be personal and tailored.

- Provide development programs for managers to improve engagement and commitment.
- Be mentored by a leader or manager who has excelled in engaging his or her employees.
- Convene a distinguished panel of managers who exhibit outstanding abilities to engage their employees. Hold this panel at company or town hall meetings and encourage people to ask questions and learn from the experts.
- Recognize and publicize managers who have mentored and developed future top performers and leaders.
- Post engagement scores by department and manager for all to see. Transparency is a form of accountability.
- Hold managers accountable for taking action on surveys and improving results.

Tools and Templates

The conclusion of each chapter will include several tools and templates that can be used to implement important themes and ideas. Please feel free to adapt these tools to your own use.

Tool 1: Segmented Engagement and Turnover Data

Summary engagement scores or turnover rates do not provide very useful information. They enable broad comparisons to competitors, but more specific categorization is needed to be able to take the right corrective actions. Especially in large organizations, summary data hide important variations that can be quite meaningful. For example, it may be that the organization's engagement scores are high except in three locations. Many third-party engagement surveys provide these types of segmented findings, unless the survey is totally anonymous. The difficulty with turnover data is to isolate the unavoidable and acceptable turnover from those employees that the company did not want to lose.

Segment	Engagement Scores	Unwanted, Avoidable Turnover Rates
Enterprise Scores		
Country-level Scores		
Business Unit-level Scores		
Location-level Scores		
Department-level Scores		
Manager Scores		
High Performer/High Potential Scores		
First 2 Years of Employee Tenure Scores		

Tool 2: Meaningful Outcome Measures

It is important to align HR activities to business outcomes and to priorities for specific business leaders. This tool lists different types of outcome measures that might be important to an organization and then asks for specific measures that are tracked by different business leaders. For example, a consumer electronics company probably values innovation above all other outcomes; and two specific measures that its CEO tracks are 1) number of patents and 2) first six months sales of new products. By uncovering this information (through interviews and conversations with leaders), HR can align its activities to ensure that these outcomes are as positive as possible

Category of Outcome Measure	Specific Outcome Measure	Key Business Leaders
Innovation		
Quality		
Productivity		
Customer Satisfaction/ Loyalty		
Learning Curve		
Competitive Differentiation		
Strategic Accomplishment		
Cost		
Efficiency		
Revenue		
Profit		
Net Promoter Score		

Tool 3: Significant Intangible Measures

As we have seen, the market valuation of a company is often largely determined by *Intangible Assets.* This tool lists various types of intangible assets, asks for specific measures and then possible linkages to individual Board members. The ties to specific Board members may not be known, but it is useful to know, for example, that the two most influential Board members are most concerned with brand credibility. Information for this tool is usually gathered by having conversations with leaders, reading investor reports and observing Board meetings. Its purpose is to ensure a close alignment between HR activities and important business outcomes.

Category of Intangible Asset	Specific Intangible Measures	Key Board Member
Brand		
Quality of Strategy		
Execution of Strategy		
Market Share		
Product Quality		
Innovation		
Leadership Readiness		
Engagement Levels of the Workforce		
Ability to Attract and Retain Talent		
Workforce Skills and Capabilities		
Quality of Partners		
Quality of Customers		

Tool 4: Stakeholder Value Analysis

Value is often in the eye of the beholder. It is very important to know what each business leader values and which measures are most meaningful. This knowledge, not only helps in aligning HR's agenda to the businesses agenda, but it also helps in communicating results and meeting expectations. It is also very easy to forget or understate the value of certain stakeholders. This tool provides a discipline to help ensure that all important stakeholders are heard and considered. It should be noted that Tools 2 and 3 in this chapter also define the linkage from outcome/intangible measures to specific leaders or Board members (i.e., stakeholders). Those tools start from the outcome or intangible measure while this tool starts with the stakeholder first.

Stakeholder	Business Priorities	Key Metrics	Communication Plan

Tool 5: Manager Scorecard

Good managers create a cycle of value and they are critical levers to stronger engagement and productivity. This tool helps to array relevant information so that good managers can be identified and leveraged. It can also assist in the coaching of less effective managers. The last two columns need some explanation. One mark of an excellent manager is the number of employees who have been promoted -both internally and externally- to desired positions. The last column pertains to organizations that operate in an open talent marketplace where employees choose to move from one manager to another. As managers get the reputation of being good to work for, they become talent magnets that attract the best talent.

Manager	Engagement Scores	Unwanted, Avoidable Turnover Rate	Number of Employees Promoted	Pipeline of Internal Moves/Transfers

Summary

The perception that HR adds no value is probably the most pervasive of all. There will continue to be biased leaders and poor HR professionals who feed into this perception, but the preponderance of evidence leads to a very different set of conclusions: With the right HR capabilities and leadership, HR programs positively impact the business, strengthen competitive advantage and position the company for stronger future success. When HR creates the context that enables talent to flourish, the force-multiplier effect leads to a cycle of value that leads the company forward and beyond.

The evidence is there. People are entitled to their own opinions, but not their own facts. And the many studies and data presented in this chapter are clear and by no means exhaustive. More and more evidence and successful practices continue to be presented each day. HR professionals need to be not just aware of these studies but be bold advocates for the role that HR can play to strengthen the workforce, workplace and company.

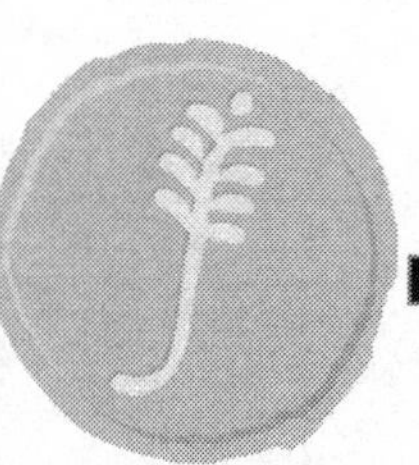

Chapter 2

Perception Two:
HR is Siloed and Too Inwardly Focused

> *"It is very easy to detect those who couch what they say in terms of the business language and priorities, as opposed to those who are pre-occupied with just HR language and functional topics."*
>
> *Priscilla Vacassin, Prudential*

Early in its history HR was, in fact, separated from the business by design. The National Cash Register Company established the first HR/personnel department in 1901 after a contentious workers strike. Employees went to HR if they got injured, had a grievance or something went wrong; and the HR office was often in another building. As the Human Resources function continued to evolve, employees went to the HR department to check their records or make adjustments to them. In these eras, HR was truly a distinct and separate administrative function.

A second possible reason why HR has been siloed for much of its history is related to the culture of the HR profession itself. Professions have cultures just like countries and companies, and the HR culture created its own lexicon, protections and barriers to entry. Many professions have similar practices. IT certainly has its own language and barriers as does the financial organization. The implicit message is that *"you can't become one of us until you know all that we know,"* and this message generally becomes stronger the more insecure the profession.

A third reason for HR's siloed mindset is that as compliance has become more complex and legally sophisticated, a degree of separation has been necessary. HR does have an important role of protecting the company, mitigating legal risk and reducing outstanding lawsuits. The average cost of various types of litigation for large companies now exceeds $120 million per year--independent of awarded judgments--and is rising at a double digit rate. The average cost of an out of court settlement for employee cases is $75,000, with the average in court settlement being $217,000. Employees win cases 63% of the time.

Overall, legal settlements are a multi-billion dollar issue, especially in the United States where costs are 4 to 9 times higher than litigation in other nations. Ultimately, this legal imbalance will impact the US's ability to compete globally.

All of these reasons have merged to create a situation in which HR is often more comfortable in its own silo, speaking its own language, retreating to processes and conversing with like-minded colleagues. This is HR's comfort zone, and as Tichy has described, there is little motivation to change or do anything differently in the comfort zone. This is particularly the case when HR professionals do not understand the business imperative for change.

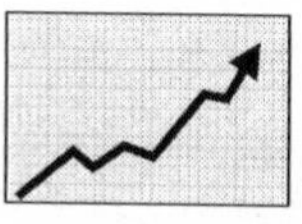

The Evidence

Given the perception and even the tendency for HR being too internally focused, it is useful to review research and thought leadership in the profession to determine if this pattern continues to exist or even becomes more entrenched. Will HR retreat into its own shell or are there indications that HR will become more closely aligned to the business? There are four lines of inquiry to review.

1. HR Stage Models
2. The Drive to Improve Business Acumen
3. Defining Strategic HR Activities
4. Changing the Past: HR Transformations

HR Stage Models

Stage Models depict sequential stages in HR's evolution as a profession. The first of three stage models to be presented is Dave Ulrich's 4P framework. HR's evolution can be viewed as going from Polite to Police to Partner to Player. He says that while HR certainly has an employee relations and compliance roles today, these Ps are not sufficient to add value to the business on a continuing basis. To do this, HR must move to the Partner and Player side of the equation.

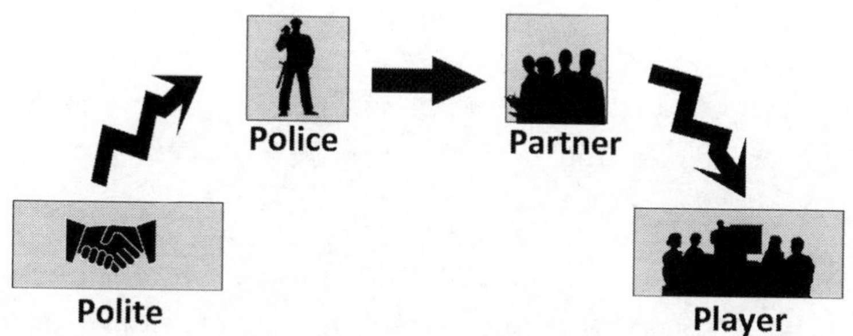

Figure 2-1: The Evolution of HR (Ulrich, 2001)

But the movement to Partner and Player requires new mindsets and skills. Ulrich acknowledges that not all HR professionals will make this transition.

He believes that 20% of the HR population is already performing strategically at the business partner and player levels; and that an equal 20% will not ever make this transition. This latter group either doesn't see the need to change or is too comfortable with their current position. The remaining 50 to 60% of HR professionals are willing to change but don't currently have the necessary skills and experiences. But this change will not be easy, given that Bersin (2013) estimates that only 15% of HR professionals receive any type of professional development.

The second stage model takes a different perspective. The Human Capital Institute (HCI) focuses on the role of HR in different economic eras, and asks the question: Is HR changing fast enough to continue to add value?

Many human resource and talent practices are anchored in a previous era and are, therefore, out of touch with today's workforce, technology, global-scope, and accelerated pace of change.

Figure 2-2: HR's Role in Different Economic Eras

During the Industrial Age, the focus was on manufacturing and making products to fuel the growth and aspirations of the American market. Henry Ford was literally the driver of this era, and both his Model T and workforce policies were trendsetters that many others would attempt to follow. Unlike the agrarian 19th century, economic advantage was gained by economies of scale and process improvements. HR was all about keeping the assembly lines moving.

In the 1950s the economy began to shift to more services than finished goods. As industries such as banking, insurance and health care came into prominence, employees did more than follow manufacturing protocols. In the Service Age, the knowledge worker was born and people became the organization's biggest potential asset. HR was all about personnel and advocating for the employees who fueled this emerging sector of the economy.

The Innovation Age was ushered into prominence in the late Twentieth Century as technology transformed businesses and personal lives. Entire industries changed, sometimes in the blink of an eye, and success required different skill sets and capabilities from the workforce. Those organizations who made this transition were very successful; those that didn't often perished. As analysts observed, there were two types of companies in these fast changing times: the quick and the dead.

The primary characteristic of the Innovation Age is the unrelenting and rapid pace of change. Businesses have to adapt, but often their internal processes are slower to respond. The key question to ask is: Is HR changing fast enough to make the business successful?

The third stage model is from Josh Bersin and Deloitte (2015) and it traces HR over a thirty year period. It identifies four stages of HR's evolution.

Stage	Personnel Department	Strategic HR	Integrated Talent Management	Business-Integrated HR
Examples of Activities	Administration Payroll Regulation Backoffice Functions	Recruiting L and D Total Rewards Service Center COE	Succession Management Coaching Leadership Integrated Talent Practices and Processes	Differentiate Talent and Roles Global Optimization of Talent Predictive Analytics
Key Role	Backoffice Functions	HR Business Partners	Talent Management	Player in the Business
Primary Emphasis	Control	Serve Staff	Enable Better Decisions	Drive the Business

Figure 2-3: The Bersin Stage Model (2015)

While all of these stage models use somewhat different terms, the message is the same: for HR to be effective going forward a new set of skills and experiences are needed. Relying on past success is not sufficient for the conditions and context of today. These models all require HR professionals to get closer to the business, take a broader perspective and become trusted and respected business leaders themselves.

The Drive to Improve Business Acumen

Business Acumen is the big picture of the organization. It includes a thorough understanding of: the value proposition of the business; its competitive positioning in the marketplace; the drivers of revenue and profit; its strategy, business goals and key initiatives; and the value provided to customers and suppliers (Cope, 2012). HR will simply not be allowed to have meaningful conversations with other business leaders until it demonstrate a thorough understanding of the business.

Recent findings by the Corporate Executive Board (CEB) reinforce the importance of business acumen for HR professionals. This study showed the HR competencies most essential to playing more of a strategic role. The following were reported.

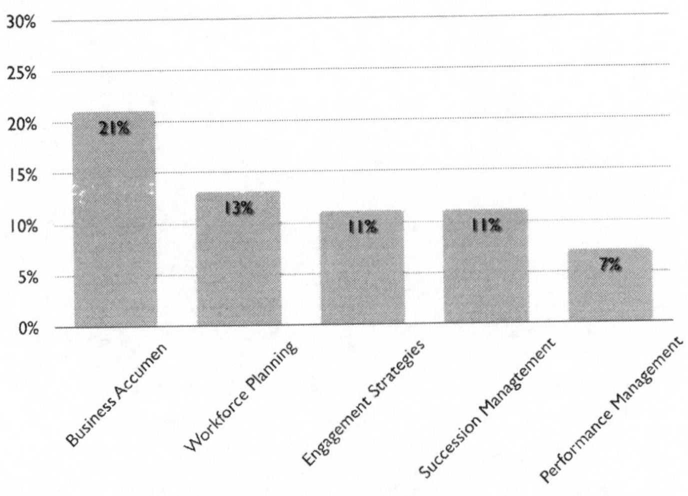

Figure 2-4: Competencies That Impact HR's Strategic Effectiveness

By a large measure, business acumen is the most important competency to demonstrate. If business acumen is not being demonstrated, HR professionals don't even get the chance to be more strategic and make other contributions.

Financial literacy is a critical component of business acumen. It is essential to understand the drivers of revenue and profit as well as the key financial statements in the business. This understanding will vary depending whether the company is public or private and the complexity of the company's value proposition.

"Every business runs on financial data. If you don't know the tools of finance, you can't put that information to work. If you can't even speak the language, you'll be left out of larger conversations about your company, and your career may suffer as well. (HBR Guide, 2012)"

Ram Charan (2001) has long counseled *"follow the money"* as a way of really understanding how a business works. In cash-based accounting businesses, such as restaurants and retail stores, this is relatively easy to do; cash is collected when a sale is made. In businesses with sales forces, partners, channels and different contracting vehicles, it can be difficult to follow the exchange of money for value. But Charan nevertheless encourages us to think like street vendors and be able to explain the business in simple, direct terms.

Business acumen is the pre-requisite to becoming a partner and player in the business. It is the table stakes, and it is the antithesis of a siloed mentality. To add more strategic value, HR professionals must become better business people, have a broader vision and be able to take actions that improve business processes and outcomes. If not, they will again be relegated to just administrative and operational roles.

Defining Strategic HR Activities

One way to characterize HR activities is to categorize them as being primarily administrative, operational or strategic in nature. As we have seen, HR does have a legacy of being more administrative (record keeping) and operational (e.g. benefits, compensation and recognition systems) than strategic. With increasing cost pressures, organizations consider outsourcing and automating functions that are administrative and operational. Self-service technology platforms are simply one example of this direction.

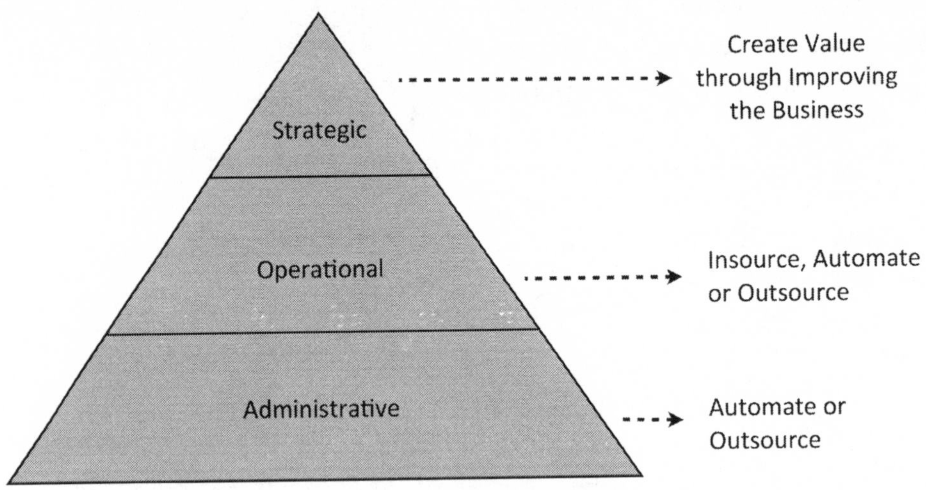

Figure 2-5: HR Segments

It is clear that the strategic area of the pyramid is where more value is exchanged, silos are broken down, greater job security exists and stronger impacts can be realized. But it can be difficult to define *"strategic"* as the term means different things to different people. Furthermore, this discussion about strategic HR has been going on for decades, and as Lawler and Boudreau (2012) have documented, HR professionals are spending only about 6 hours per week on strategic activities, and this figure has not changed in twenty years.

So with all the emphasis on being more strategic, why has the profession been slow to adopt new practices? There are certainly many contributing factors, including:

- Change is hard to accomplish and many HR professionals either do not want to or do not have the right skills to provide more strategic value.
- People believe they are doing strategic work, but are not.
- Technology is needed to reduce operational burdens and free time for more strategic activities.
- It is not simply the amount of time being spent on strategic activities but the effectiveness of that time that matters most.
- Business leaders are not asking for HR to be more strategic.

Lawler and Boudreau address the definitional issue of what being strategic actually means. In a SHRM publication they identify 6 questions that HR professionals should ask themselves about their strategic role.

1. How do you manage talent?
2. How do you engage in strategic business activities?
3. What is your HR strategy?
4. How well do you measure HR efficiency?
5. How well do you measure HR effectiveness?
6. How well do you measure impact?

The authors, like others, see talent management as a strategic activity. They also see participating in strategic activities such as planning and workforce segmentation as qualifying as strategic actions. And finally, Lawler and Boudreau place a heavy emphasis on evidence and measurement-driven analysis. They distinguish among three types of outcomes: efficiency, effectiveness and impact. Lawler and Boudreau believe that HR has emphasized efficiency, whereas the business is much more interested in effectiveness and impact.

HCI has also defined strategic HR and it encompasses both mindsets and activities. Their set of strategic characteristics includes:

- Seeing the big picture, understanding the industry and strengthening future competitive advantage.
- Becoming a stronger business person, knowing what is important to the business and how different parts of the organization, including but not restricted to HR, contribute value.
- Leveraging talented employees so that the right people with the right skills are in the right job at the right time.
- Using data, evidence and insights to mitigate organizational risk and strengthen performance.
- Solving business problems.
- Improving business results through better alignment, cost savings and productivity improvements.

HCI's characteristics include the talent management and data-driven criteria listed by Lawler and Boudreau. But what is interesting about HCI's list is that the words *Human Resources* or the abbreviation *HR* does not appear. All of these strategic characteristics are stated in business terminology (and not HR language).

Karen Hilton, a Senior Vice President of HR for TRX, presented at the 2013 HCI conference on Strategic Workforce Planning. Her talk was entitled *"The Look and Feel of Strategic HR."* Her recommendations are based on her considerable experience, and while she reinforces some criteria mentioned by others, she adds some important new insights and behaviors.

The Look and Feel of Strategic HR
• Makes recommendations, analysis and insights based on business-centric data. • Links initiatives to outcomes that matter to the Income Statement or Balance Sheet. • Uses a decision framework of Strategy-Issues-Measures-Outcomes (SIMO) to ensure that the right issues are being addressed. • Is well versed in industry, organizational and competitive landscape issues. • Is accountable at the same standard and level as other business functions. • Interacts with stakeholders courageously. • Acts boldly.

Figure 2-6: The Look and Feel of Strategic HR (Hilton, 2013)

Hilton's contributions are the SIMO framework which helps to align HR activities to strategy and strategic initiatives; and the bold point of view that she espouses. She believes it is time for HR to stand up and be heard.

While there is growing consensus on what strategic means, there continues to be a question about the value provided by these more strategic services. Do they make any discernable difference? The Corporate Leadership Council

(CLC), a leading consulting and research organization, addressed this specific question. Their research focused on the impact of improving strategic HR activities and linkages to outcomes. Their findings show that more strategic HR activities lead to:

- ✓ 21% improvement in employee performance
- ✓ 26% improvement in employee retention
- ✓ 7% increase in revenue
- ✓ 9% increase in profitability

Ulrich and Brockbank (2005) also examined the impact of various HR competencies on business performance. Their findings show a similar pattern.

Competency Category	HR Effectiveness (1 low to 5 high)	Impact on Business Performance
Strategic Contribution	3.65	43%
Personal Credibility	4.13	23%
HR Delivery	3.69	16%
Business Knowledge	3.44	11%
HR Technology	3.02	5%

Figure 2-7: HR's Impact on Business (Ulrich and Brockbank, 2005)

This research underscores the importance of HR making a strategic contribution. Furthermore, it indicates that what HR professionals do best (personal credibility) has only modest influence on the business; while what HR does moderately well (making a strategic contribution) has almost twice the influence (or more) on the business than any other competency.

Changing the Past: HR Transformations

We have seen the tendency of the HR profession to be more internally focused and even isolationist. There are historical and psychological reasons for this stance, but the world is a different place now and there are increasing pressures on the profession to break out of this pattern. HR stage models trumpet the new demands of the Innovation Age and Business Integrated HR. Increasingly, improving Business Acumen is seen as essential for understanding the business more thoroughly, and the pathway for HR professionals to be accepted by their business counterparts. And as HR becomes more data-driven and committed to improving business processes and outcomes, then its strategic role will be more appreciated and expected.

Now, the question remains, are HR departments making these types of changes: are they becoming more externally-focused, solution-centric, taking a broader perspective and dedicated to improving business outcomes? There are several sources of evidence to suggest that the HR profession is changing in precisely these ways.

1. KPMG Research "Rethinking Human Resources in a Changing World" (2012)

70% of HR organizations are going through significant changes. While there may be many reasons for this activity, it cannot all be attributed to cost savings and process improvements. The 2012 KPMG study done in conjunction with The Economist observes that *"There clearly remains a vast gulf between the perceived importance and perceived effectiveness of HR today."* Organizations are taking actions to address this gap, be crisper about communicating value, focus more on strategic services and be more data-driven and outcomes focused.

2. Fed Ex: From Bricklayer to Architect.

FedEx has over 300,000 employees worldwide, serves 220 countries, handles a volume of 10 million packages a day, has a fleet of over 660 aircraft, is regularly recognized as a best place to work and records more than $45B in annual revenues. FedEx is a very successful organization but is always looking for ways to continue to be more successful in the workplace and marketplace. Looking at their own data, FedEx knows that increasing customer loyalty by 1% adds $100 million in incremental revenue. This is a very significant business finding, and the question now becomes: what levers does HR have to impact this result?

Based on the research of James Heskett and the experience of other leading companies such as Southwest Airlines, FedEx understands that marketplace success is built on workplace success. FedEx undertook a major initiative to change the focus and direction of the HR organization. Bob Bennet, a FedEx vice president, outlined a series of changes that moved HR from being a Bricklayer to an Architect.

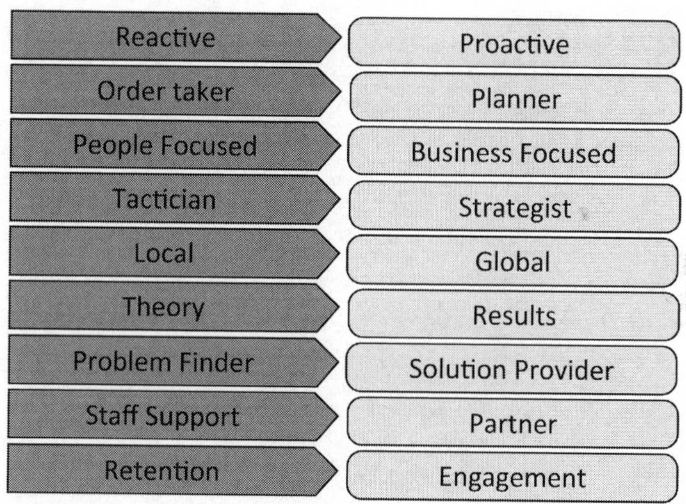

Figure 2-8: HR at FedEx: From Bricklayer to Architect (2012)

It is again important to emphasize that the Bricklayer role is important; its lays the foundation for many useful operational activities. But in today's rapidly changing world, operational success is not enough. HR professional must now be forward looking, anticipatory and business-driven.

3. IBM

IBM is one of the world's most respected brands and companies. It is truly a global company with over 350,000 employees worldwide, with the majority being outside the United States. IBM has also recognized the need for change in the HR function. Distinctions are drawn between the traditional and emerging paradigm, and the abbreviation TM in the Emerging Paradigm refers to Talent Management.

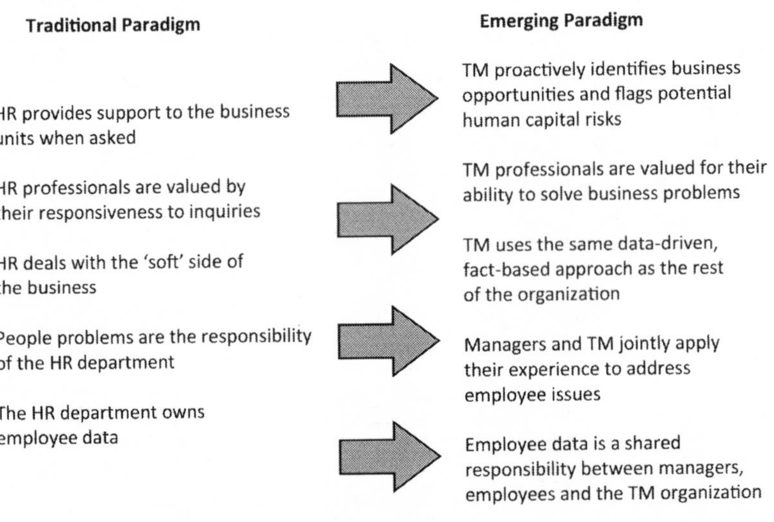

Traditional Paradigm
Emerging Paradigm
HR provides support to the business units when asked
TM proactively identifies business opportunities and flags potential human capital risks
HR professionals are valued by their responsiveness to inquiries
TM professionals are valued for their ability to solve business problems
HR deals with the 'soft' side of the business
TM uses the same data-driven, fact-based approach as the rest of the organization
People problems are the responsibility of the HR department
Managers and TM jointly apply their experience to address employee issues
The HR department owns employee data
Employee data is a shared responsibility between managers, employees and the TM organization

Figure 2-9: Traditional and Emerging HR Models, IBM Institute for Business Value

Notice the words used in the emerging paradigm: business opportunities, risks, solving business problems, data-driven and fact-based. These, again, are not characteristic of a siloed HR perspective; they are business terms and concepts that HR leaders are expected to embrace.

4. CHROs from Different Functions

While it is difficult to gather precise data on the career paths of Chief Human Resource Officers (CHROs), there are now many examples of CHROs from other disciplines or HR professionals who have served on cross-functional assignments to deepen and broaden their perspectives. The *"straight line"* path up through only the HR silo seems to be less prevalent because CEOs value business acumen, operational mindsets, and real-world business decision-making experience.

Deloitte (2015) has recognized this trend in its *"Global Human Capital Trends 2015."* It states that nearly 40% of new Chief Human Resource Officers come from operational and other business functions. This will not be the last time that this topic of the best preparation for leading the HR function will arise. It is actually a very spirited debate, with some very practical guidelines emerging. Deloitte goes on to recognize how the CHRO role is changing.

> *"In this era of rapid business change, the role of the CHRO becomes radically different and more demanding than ever. Today's CHRO must be innovative and business-savvy and be able to stand toe to toe with the CEO. At the same time, a CHRO must know how to bring the HR team together and help it evolve into a more distributed, business-integrated function. CHROs must also be comfortable adopting and embracing technology and analytics, which are integral to HR's future success."*
>
> *Deloitte*

5. Dave Ulrich: HR From the Outside, In

When Dave Ulrich and his colleagues at RBL (Results Based Leadership) work with HR organizations, they start with a simple question: Tell us about your business. They use this question as a litmus test for the HR function and the value it likely contributes. If the responses are about the HR business and not the business of the business, then it may be a very long day.

Ulrich believes that HR adds value from the outside, in; and not the other way around. They believe that the external, *outside-in* approach consists of a deep understanding of three interrelated factors: 1) the business context and industry, 2) the specific stakeholders that shape the business, and 3) the company-specific strategy and its competitive positioning. HR cannot possibly add value outside-in with a siloed mindset.

> *"If HR professionals are truly to contribute to business performance, then their mindset must center on the goals of the business. They must take that outside reality and bring it into everything they do, practicing their craft with an eye to the business as a whole and not just their own department."*
>
> *Ulrich, Younger, Brockbank and Ulrich, 2012*

Recommendations and Insights:

1. A Different Zeitgeist is Coming.

It takes time to escape the past, recognize the changing demands of the future and develop a new world view. The HR profession is at that inflection point for many of the past perceptions that have characterized it. In the previous chapter, the view that HR adds no value to the business was challenged. The evidence is clear, and has been for almost two decades, but the view persists. It has taken a generation of more information, better research, stronger examples, new leaders and different mindsets for attitudes to shift. The same is true for the belief that HR is too process-driven, unresponsive, lives in its own silo and speaks its own language.

Part of the fuel for HR being accepted as a more integral part of the organization is a growing emphasis on collaboration among groups and departments of a company. This has long been the curse of CEOs in large organizations: They have all these smart people, but they don't synchronize well. There are now many examples of the positive impacts of breaking down barriers, getting people to work together, using social media to form new connections (crowdsourcing) and benefit from what GE calls a *"boundaryless"* organization. This drive for greater collaboration and leverage from leaders, plus the new generations in the workforce being so comfortable searching out and establishing new connections, has set a great context for HR to break out of its own silo.

The result of these drivers and the sheer weight of research, models and best practices is that HR is moving to partner and player status. It is becoming more business-focused, because that is what all groups and departments must do. HR is no different in this regard; but it is probably the clearest example of a group that has been out of synch.

2. Follow the Money

Ram Charan and Deep Throat are right: it's all about the money. There is no better way to demonstrate business acumen and enhance credibility with colleagues than by becoming knowledgeable about three key financial statements: The Income Statement, Balance Sheet and Cash Flow Analysis. These financial statements are typically way out of the comfort zone of HR professionals who are thought to be *"good with words but not numbers."* But money is the language of the business, and it is extremely important to be conversant with these three key financial statements.

There are several readily-available sources for financial information. If you work in a publically-traded company, the 10K filings are available and easy to access. The notes and commentary in the 10K report can be particularly valuable. There are a number of external financial sites such as Hoovers and Bloomberg news that also have business information for review. It can also be extremely useful to listen to the quarterly earnings calls with analysts. The information presented in these calls is interesting but so are the questions that get asked of company leaders. Finally, connect with a financial buddy who can walk you through reports and financial information.

It is important to realize that HR professionals do not need to run right out and get their Masters in Finance to be credible. HR professionals do not have to be experts in finance, but they do need to speak the language, be able to read the important reports, ask the right questions and take actions to improve the financial picture. They need to understand the big four financial concepts: Revenue, profit, assets and cash and the levers that HR has to improve financial outcomes.

Perhaps the two most valuable financial literacy skills are: 1) ability to review a financial statement and recognize the story that it tells, and 2) ask the right questions to gain more insight. For example, if an Income Statement is reviewed, it is relatively easy to determine if:

- Revenue growth or decline over several years, including the percentage increase or decrease
- Cost, both direct and overhead, are growing or declining and by what percentage
- Gross and net profit increase or decline

Once this information has been gathered, then it is important to discern the bigger picture (the story). For example, it could be that a company is profitable, but that costs are growing faster than revenues over a several year period of time. This situation should then lead to several questions that can provide even more insight, including:

- Which costs are growing faster? COGS (cost of goods sold which is the direct cost of providing the product or service) or SG&A (sales, general and administrative which is the overhead line)?
- How does the revenue increases compare with others in our industry?
- Are some products growing at a faster rate than others?

These types of questions lead to better, more informed findings and judgments. These are the types of discussions that HR professionals can engage in and ones that make a difference to the business. Follow the money so the right problems can be fixed.

3. **Mindsets Matter.**

HR professionals must believe that they are business people first. This view is not abandoning the HR profession. It is the realization of how HR professionals can add the most value both to their organizations and careers.

A part of HR's silo-mentality is engrained in the profession itself. It is self-inflicted. HR is in its comfort zone, but this doesn't matter to the people that matter most. Seth Godin, the influential marketing leader, states that value in this new age is all about connections. The people with more connections, win; and the irony is that HR should not mildly resist leaving its own silo but actively demand it. HR should become the network-builder and community-maker itself; it should be the glue that holds the organization together. But to do so, HR must believe in itself, have a strong point of view and be willing to take risk.

4. The Cobbler's Children.

It has been established that HR needs to act differently. This fact is recognized by business leaders and HR itself. Even when HR adds value, it does a poor job of articulating this value to others and to itself. KPMG (2014) research says that while 60% of leaders expect HR to grow in strategic significance, only 17% say that HR does a good job of demonstrating its value to the business.

For HR to become more business-driven and strategic, three things must happen. First, HR must be given the chance to escape its past and play this role. As we have seen, this opportunity, after years of anticipation, is increasingly open to HR professionals today. Second, HR professionals need new skills and capabilities to consistently perform at the strategic level. In Part II of *Fearless HR,* a new HR Capabilities Framework is presented that can hopefully guide this effort. But HR must start to invest in itself to witness the type of return that can make a rapid impact. And third, HR must believe in itself and develop a strong point of view that is credible and respected within the organization.

Tools and Templates

The purpose of these tools and templates is to broaden HR's perspective, help to ensure a more business-focused approach, promote a closer alignment between the business and HR, and move beyond the HR silo. .

Tool 1: Strategic Focus

The first step in taking the broader perspective of the business is to be able to identify the major points of connection and move beyond generalities. While many people will say they know the strategy and goals of the company, it is another thing to be able to document them. This tool can be completed by referencing annual reports, company documents, external sources or interviewing leaders. The Values/Cultural Attributes entry is important because for organizations such as P&G, FedEx and Branson companies, the values become key drivers for business decisions.

Focus Area	Definition / Description
Strategy	
Business Goal	
Values/Culture Attributes	
Strategic Initiatives	

Tool 2: External Factors

There are a variety of external factors that can impact the strategy and direction of the company. While these external factors cannot be controlled, they can be anticipated and understood. This tool is very useful in building business acumen, understanding the larger context that impacts the business and escaping a siloed mentality. Consider having HR teams fill out this tool, not just for the company as a whole, but for separate divisions as well.

External Factors	Impacts
Political Factors	
Economic Conditions	
Market Dynamics	
Technology Innovations	
Legal Policies and Government Actions	
Social Patterns/Lifestyle	
Environmental Impacts	
Security Challenges	
Demographic Factors	
Competitive Threats	

Tool 3: Competitive Differentiation Map: Example and Tool

This tool is adapted from Boudreau and Ramstad (2007) and its purpose is to provide clarity about the specifics of how your company differs from its primary competitors. This is an excellent tool to build business acumen, industry understanding and competitive positioning knowledge. It is not sustainable in today's economy to have a *"me-too"* competitive strategy, and by understanding the specific competitive differentiators, HR can help to maximize strengths and narrow weaknesses.

An Example: This Competitive Differentiation Map is for two companies in the *jewelry retail business.* The specific ways in which they compete are detailed in column 1.

Differentiators	Company 1	Company 2
Customer service	High	Low to Moderate
Product variety	Focused	Great
Product quality	High	Mixed
Size of store	Small	Large
Store locations	Limited	Many
Use of technology	Low	High

In this example, Company 1 is a local jeweler with several stores, has products tailored to its clientele and offers very personal and responsive customer service. In all likelihood, the owners know your name, have serviced your family for decades and are respected craftsmen. Company 2 is a big box jewelry story with many locations, a great variety of products, and you are likely serviced by a sales person on commission.

While the two companies seem very similar—they are both in the jewelry business--these competitive differences are extremely important to decisions about talent and success in both the workplace and marketplace.

Complete the Competitive Differentiation Tool for your major competitors. Talk to business, operational and marketing colleagues to complete this exercise, and then work with your team to identify the HR levers to improve this map.

Competitive Differentiation Map

Differentiators	My Company	Competitor 1	Competitor 2

Tool 4: SWOT Analysis Example and Tool

The SWOT Analysis is a very popular strategic planning tool. The acronym stands for Strengths, Weaknesses, Opportunities and Threats. Because SWOT is so widely used, it is an excellent tool for HR professionals to improve their business acumen, strategic awareness and business literacy.

An Example: The following SWOT analysis was performed on a company. A team was assembled and they brainstormed each quadrant and then prioritized the top four/five factors. The Internal Factors column can be controlled or modified by the company (not easily but actions can be taken). The External Factors can not be directly influenced by company actions, but contingency plans must be prepared to mitigate future risks

Internal Factors	**External Factors**
Strengths • Cash • Employee skills • Brand • Global presence • Existing customer base	**Opportunities** • Evolving and open markets • MINT economies and growing global markets • Partnerships • Converging technologies
Weaknesses • New product track record • Innovative leadership • Incorporating acquisitions • Aging technology platforms for products • Complacent culture	**Threats** • Three major competitors • Emerging new competitors • Changing consumer preferences • Political instability and economic downturn

What story does this SWOT example tell?

This SWOT tells the story of a company that has been successful in the past but is struggling developing new sources of revenue. It is a company living off its past successes. The most telling quadrant is Weaknesses: new products and innovations are underperforming. Market conditions change all the time, but it is reasonable to suggest that companies such as Kodak, Sony, Blockbuster, RIM, Sears and even Microsoft might fit this picture.

Complete the SWOT Analysis for your own company. Enlist others in this project.

The SWOT Analysis

Internal	External
Strengths	**Opportunities**
Weaknesses	**Threats**

Tool 5: SWOT Analysis Action Guide

The SWOT Analysis cannot only improve your business acumen and literacy, it can help to align and set the HR agenda. If the SWOT Analysis identifies the factors that can most influence the business—good or bad—then these factors should be part of HR's agenda as well. A critical aspect of alignment is that HR is taking the perspective and priorities of the business. Furthermore, the 4Ms of maximize, magnify, minimize and mitigate are excellent conversations to have with business unit leaders. As these leaders see the HR levers to improve the SWOT picture, this lends credibility to HR's role and contributions.

Internal	**External**
Strengths *Maximize*	**Opportunities** *Magnify*
Weaknesses *Minimize*	**Threats** *Mitigate*

Tool 6: HR Cross-Functional Buddies

One way to get a broader perspective and bust out of silos is to have colleagues within different groups. In Part II of *Fearless HR*, these cross-functional relationships will be termed *"bridging networks."* The term *"buddy"* is used because these relationships are not part of a reporting structure but rather among colleagues who can contribute value to each other. It is a reciprocal relationship that builds visibility and capability.

Department or Group	Person	Areas of Expertise and Interest
Finance		
Information Technology		
Operations-Local		
Operations-Domestic		
Operations-Global		
Branding		
Social Media		
Legal and Compliance		
Marketing		
Sales		
R and D		
Customer Service		
HR Business Partner		
HR Central Functions		

SUMMARY

HR has certainly existed in its own silo. In its early years, workers left the production floor if they had to go to HR. HR itself also contributed to a silo mentality by using jargon, arcane processes and other artificial barriers to *"keep people out."* But as the economy has changed, so have expectations and requirements. An inward focus for HR, perhaps once a strength, is now a major weakness. HR simply cannot provide strategic value from its own silo.

HR is more outwardly focused because it is embedded in the business. HR's goals are not just about improving HR, but increasingly they are focused on improving the business. New HR professionals are reaching out to establish relationships with colleagues from throughout the organization, not just their own department. Business leaders look to HR to be able to manage the turbulent change that impacts both the workplace and workforce,; and to create the context in which talent can flourish. Increasingly CEOs are looking to CHROs as one of the three or four most important members of the executive team. And as HR leaders move from being partners to players, the *silo-mentality* is being replaced by the *business-mentality.*

Chapter 3

Perception Three: HR is a Weak Discipline with Poor Tools

> *"Most organizations make decisions about their people's talents and how those people are organized with far less rigor, logic and distinctiveness than their decisions about other resources, like money and technology."*
>
> *Boudreau and Ramstad, 2007*

HR is perceived as a soft discipline. One reason for this perception is that the tools and methodologies for hard disciplines such as engineering, logistics and manufacturing are more mature and easier to understand, visualize and describe. In manufacturing, for example, ways to improve production efficiencies have been in practice for decades with the re-engineering, lean six sigma and total quality practices (TQM) from the 1960s. Furthermore, these approaches have entire infrastructures built around them including training, certifications, graduate degrees and personal designations such as yellow and black belts.

Boudreau and Ramstad (2007) have examined the basis for talent decisions in organizations. Many of these decisions have been made by intuition and preference, instead of evidence and strategic direction. They further determined that talent decisions are usually made based on one of four rationales.

1. **Compliance:** This approach makes the argument that rules, regulations and standards must be followed because penalties and fees will result if deviations occur. In some cases this approach may be more of a threat than an actual reality; but the average cost of litigation can be very intimidating. The *"police"* role of HR, when obsessively followed, can contribute to the perception that HR is too process-driven.

2. **Fads and Fashions:** Talent decisions can be unduly influenced by the practices of other companies, especially if they are admired organizations. Remember the old adage: *"no one ever got fired for recommending IBM, or for doing succession planning like GE, or for collaborating like Google."* There is, however, a danger in blindly applying other practices to your company without modification. It can be easy to forget, for example, that the GE talent calibration system was also used at Enron.

3. **Equality:** *"Let's treat everyone the same."* This is perhaps the most frequent talent rationale, because it is easy to implement and seems fair. It is true that all employees are important and must be treated fairly, honestly and with respect. But the authors make the distinction between equality (treating everyone the same) and equity (treatment based on value provided). For decades marketing departments have been segmenting customers on the value they provide. This doesn't mean that all customers aren't important because they are; but it is a reality that some customers contribute more value. The equality criterion, then, seems fair but is actually short-changing the business.

4. **Strategic Logic:** This is the ultimate criterion, and the way that talent decisions should be evaluated. There should be a meaningful and direct *"line of sight"* from strategy to talent activities for each organization. This approach precludes just using compliance, fads and equality as primary bases for talent decisions. There should be close alignment between HR initiatives and an organization's strategy, competitive positioning, strategic initiatives and business goals.

> *"Building competitive advantage requires the right workforce strategy, but that does not mean simply putting people first. It means* ***putting strategy first*** *and developing a workforce that executes that strategy."*
>
> *Becker, Huselid and Beatty, 2009*

John Boudreau has further described what he calls *Decision Sciences.* He frames this discussion around three professions: sales/marketing, accounting/finance and HR. He distinguishes between professional practices and decision sciences, the former being internal activities that improve efficiency of each practice, while the latter are guidelines for spending resources to improve outcomes and impacts. In the broad discipline of finance, for example, a professional practice would be to streamline accounts receivable while the decision science of finance would be to differentiate the types of business returns on capital invested. Professional practices are often about control and efficiency while decisions sciences are about optimization and impacts.

Boudreau discusses the maturity of the professions of sales/marketing, finance and HR. While accounting has a 500 year history and sales is arguably the oldest profession, HR is a relative newcomer with only a hundred year tradition. It is understandable, then, that HR decision models are not as advanced or sophisticated. Using sales/marketing as an example, Boudreau describes the role of Alfred Sloan in the 1920s as targeting various GM brands to different market segments. Chevrolets were targeted to the midmarket, not Cadillacs; and this had major ramifications for branding, communications, and product life cycle management.

In HR, the professional practice is operational HR and the decision science is strategic HR. Furthermore, Boudreau states that organizations that are on the tipping point of moving from professional practices to decision sciences enjoy a competitive advantage over industry cohorts slower to react.

> *"The ability to make good decisions about people represents one of the last reliable sources of competitive advantage, since so few organizations are very good at it."*
>
> *Peter Drucker*

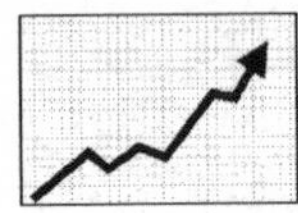

THE EVIDENCE

The perception is that HR has poor decision frameworks and models. Let's examine the models that exist and determine if this perception is justified. There are different types of HR methodologies and frameworks. Some frameworks are *descriptive* in that they help to organize information in a clear, concise manner. Some methodologies are *sequential* in that they show relationships among various practices and suggest an order of occurrence. Some models are *predictive* in that they can provide indicators of what will likely happen. All of these types of models and methodologies can provide value and clarity.

There is also a difference between HR frameworks and business frameworks. Boudreau (2010) argues strongly for HR embracing business models that are already being used by the business. He cites examples of segmentation, product life cycle management, risk analysis, supply chain management, competitive differentiation, workforce planning and performance optimization. His suggestion makes great sense, but this does not mean that HR frameworks are not valuable themselves.

Let's review nine different frameworks and models that pertain to HR. Some are business models and some have been created by HR professionals. Each is discussed in terms of its key features and how it can be used to make more meaningful talent decisions.

1. The HCI Strategic Talent Management Model

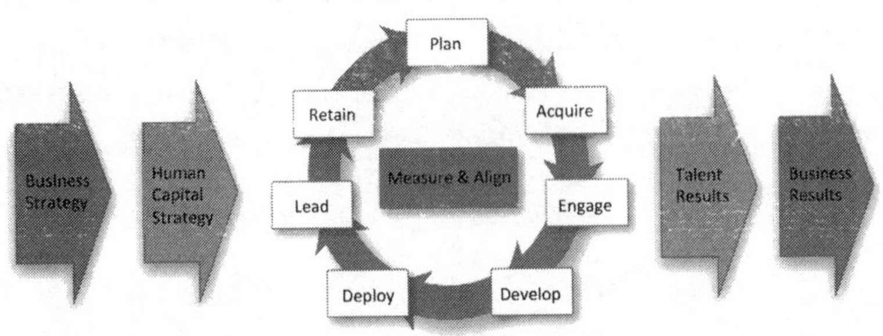

Figure 3-1: The HCI Strategic Talent Management Model

The HCI Strategic Talent Management model was first developed in 2005, and was influenced by the work of Jac Fitz-enz. There are several characteristics of this model that make it useful in making decisions about talent.

- Strategy is the driver of talent practices (the left-most arrows). If, for example, a company has technology leadership as a competitive strategy, then this strategy has direct bearing on who is hired, what type of development opportunities are provided and what the most crucial roles are.

- Talent practices in the wheel are not described in terms of HR practices (e.g., performance management or succession planning) but rather in terms and stages that employees understand. This language is clear and makes sense to the business people who use this model.

- It makes the point that the talent practices in the wheel need to work together and not be isolated activities. The wheel is about an ***integrated*** system of talent practices, not separate and distinct actions.

- The purpose of talent practices is to achieve business results (the right-most arrows); it is not about the talent practices themselves but the results and impacts they produce.

The HCI Strategic Talent Management Model has face validity with business leaders: it makes sense to them and it emphasizes the key ideas that talent practices are strategy driven, and talent practices must be an integrated system that leads to improved business results.

2. The Human Capital Value Chain

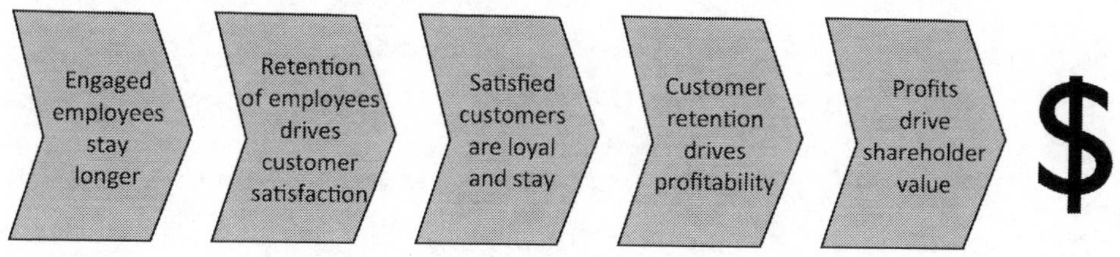

Figure 3-2: The Human Capital Value Chain

This framework is based on the work of James Heskitt and Laurie Bassi previously described. Essentially, the value chain is as follows:

- The greatest predictor of improved financial results is customer loyalty.
- A strong predictor of customer loyalty is customer satisfaction.
- A strong predictor of customer satisfaction is retention of key employees that deliver service to the customer.
- A strong predictor of key employee retention is key employee engagement.

This framework is being used to make decisions about improving business results by creating the right environment and atmosphere for employees. It clearly shows the relationship among employee engagement, customer engagement and business outcomes. It also says that to be successful in the marketplace, you must first be successful in the workplace. While the Human Capital Value Chain linkages are relevant for all types of organizations, it is most applicable to businesses with direct employee-customer interactions.

3. Talent Strategies for Building Capability: The 7B Equation

There are a variety of ways to fill organizational talent gaps, and each technique has its own strengths and weaknesses. All too often, organizations rush to fill gaps instead of thinking what should happen for the organization to be successful in both the short and longer terms. In *"Talent on Demand,"* Peter Cappelli (2008) describes the talent supply chain in uncertain times and how organizations need to balance the *Make and Buy* decisions to minimize risks of being wrong. As he correctly points out, it is not *Make or Buy*; because both strategies are required in today's turbulent world.

Dave Ulrich and colleagues have used other terms to describe ways to fill talent needs. Their 6B framework has been widely used; and while several of the Bs have changed names over the years, the current rendition is as follows:

- Buy: Recruiting, sourcing and securing new talent into the organization.
- Build: Helping people grow through on the job experiences, learning from others, training and life experiences.

- Borrow: Bringing knowledge into the organization through advisors, partners, consultants, or suppliers. This also applies to opensourcing models using the web as a source for ideas and talent.
- Boost: Promoting the right people into key jobs.
- Bounce: Removing poor performers from their jobs or the company.
- Bind: Retaining top talent through recognition, compensation and rewards.

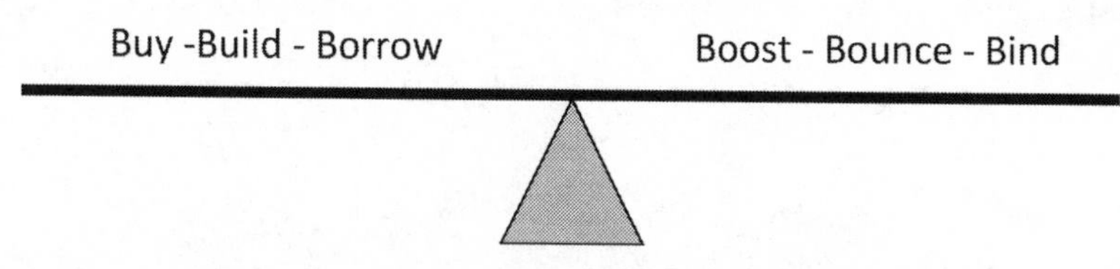

Figure 3-3: The 7 B Equation for Building Capability

When these 6 Bs are put into an equation, it leads to the question of what is the right *"balance"* of these various talent strategies. This seventh B (balance) actually becomes the most important decision fulcrum. The two most popular examples of talent decisions using the 7B equation are 1) what is the right mix of employees and contingent workers? and 2) what is the right percentage of building versus buying future leaders in the organization? There is no single correct answer to these questions as conditions vary, but the first step in answering these questions is to ascertain what the current mix is. Then, the next step can be taken by asking what the right balance ***should be*** to minimize risk and enhance success.

4. Talent Deployment Framework: The 6Rs

Jim Collins' metaphor of *"putting the right people in the right seats on the bus"* has led to a more fully featured decision framework. Major organizations today use the Rs—whether it is 4, 5 or 6Rs—as the way they assign and deploy talent. The 6Rs stand for: right people, with the right skills in the right job (alignment and fit); and at the right time, place and cost (the best investment and most practical). The 6R Framework is virtually synonymous with the practice and science of talent management itself. Pepsi, Accenture and McDonalds are among the leading companies that actively use the 6Rs to leverage talent within their organizations.

The most frequent 6R discussions are around *the right people in the right job.* This *"fit"* must be monitored and questioned on a regular basis. All too often very good people are in jobs because it is convenient or comfortable, not because it optimizes their impact and growth. Similarly, jobs that are extremely critical to company success may be staffed with low to mid-level performers (see Tools later in this chapter that address this situation). Neither situation is optimal or even acceptable. Also as organizations become truly global, the *Right Place* becomes an essential R as well as the balance between expatriate and local national staffing options.

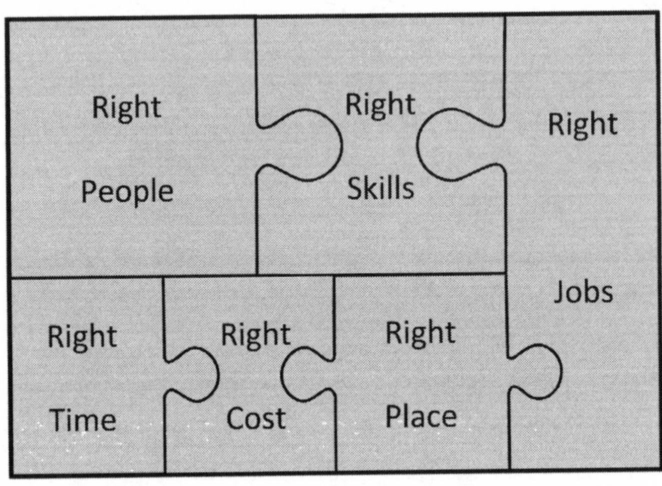

Figure 3-4: The 6 R Talent Deployment Framework

5. Strategic Workforce Planning Methodology

Strategic Workforce Planning (SWP) is one of the least mature talent practices. It has evolved from manpower planning and forecasting to consider different futures in a VUCA (volatility, uncertainty, complexity and ambiguity) world. Taken from the military, VUCA is now used to describe the various types of situations that can shake and topple organizations and even industries. Consider the following examples of change discussed by Thomas Friedman.

> *"Uber, the world's largest taxi company, owns no vehicles. Facebook, the world's most popular media owner, creates no content. Alibaba, the most valuable retailer, has no inventory. And Airbnb, the world's largest accommodation provider, owns no real estate. Something interesting is happening."*
>
> *Thomas Friedman, The New York Times, May 20, 2015*

Forecasting and operational workforce planning do little good in times of turbulent change because they merely extend the current state into the future. New SWP methodologies were needed to help organizations *"see around corners,"* mitigate risks and prepare for different possible futures.

The HCI Strategic Workforce Planning Methodology was developed in 2010. Like all workforce planning models, it compares the current state to a future state, identifying gaps and then taking action to close the gaps. The HCI model has several other important features.

- Strategy drives the methodology.
- The time horizon is typically 3 to 5 years.
- The goal is to prepare the workforce to execute the company's strategy and strategic initiatives.
- All roles in the workforce are important but all do not provide the same value. A role segmentation spectrum is defined to include strategic, core, supportive and mis-aligned roles.
- The environmental scan provides a disciplined way to examine internal and external factors that impact the workforce, key roles and strategy execution
- Different futures are defined based on possible internal and external factors, not simply best or worst case scenarios.
- The 7B framework for building capabilities is incorporated into action planning.

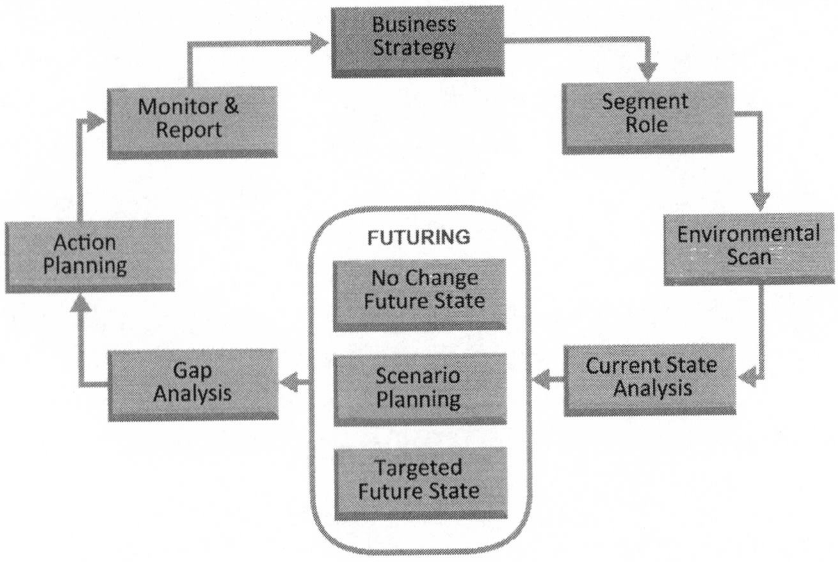

Figure 3-5: The HCI Strategic Workforce Planning Methodology

The HCI Model has been used by hundreds of public and private organizations to anticipate different futures, segment the workforce and mitigate potential risk. These decisions helped to ensure readiness, optimize the impact of talent and make the best use of scarce resources.

6. Workforce Alignment Framework

An outcome from workforce planning is an aligned workforce. This alignment is depicted in Figure 3-6.

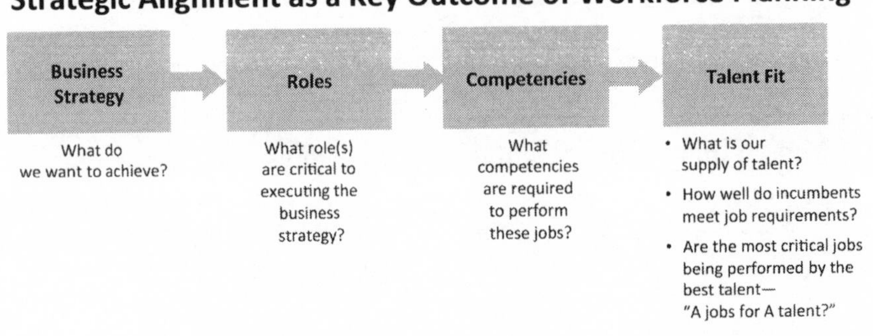

Figure 3-6: An Aligned Workforce Framework

This framework, which uses the first two steps in the Strategic Workforce Planning Model, is useful because it rectifies the perception that HR decisions about talent are based on favor, influence and intuition. This framework stipulates that people decisions are based on strategy and structure first, and only then can talent fit be entered into the equation. The Workforce Alignment Framework is an excellent example of the Boudreau and Ramstad strategic logic criterion for making talent decisions.

The distinctive aspects of the Aligned Workforce Framework are the following.

- The framework's purpose is to specify the workforce that can execute the company's strategy both now and in the future.

- Among the strategy and business drivers for the framework are 1) the company's strategy, 2) competitive differentiation from major competitors, 3) strategic initiatives such as technology implementations, mergers or reorganizations and 4) major business goals.

- Roles (groups of jobs) within the organization are segmented based on the strategic value they provide. This segmentation enables a focus on these roles and more resources being devoted to them because they return the most value. The SWP methodology uses a four role categorization of: strategic, core, supporting and misaligned. These categories are further defined in the Tool section of this chapter.

- The competencies define excellent performance within a role. It is often not enough, for example, just to stipulate that engineers are a strategic role. It is necessary to specify the 4 to 6 capabilities and qualities that these engineers should demonstrate. Boudreau (2010) reinforces the importance of this step in discussing the strategic role of engineers in the Boeing 787 Dreamliner project. It was thought the composite technical skills were the most essential skills for this role, but it turns out that relationship management skills became more vital as the project unfolded.

- The Talent Fit step is made possible by careful thought in the previous three steps. The Talent Fit is also when the 7B equation is employed, especially if the internal talent supply is inadequate.

7. Decisions Pertaining to Specific Talent Practices

There are also talent-specific frameworks that lead to better decisions about the development, growth and deployment of people. These are not really methodologies, but rather a way to summarize research, evidence and best practices so that talent decisions are consistent with the current body of knowledge. Three examples of these talent-specific frameworks are presented.

a. Motivations

Daniel Pink in his book *"Drive: The Surprising Truth in What Motivates Us"* (2009) challenges the conventional wisdom that higher financial incentives lead to greater performance. This *"carrots and sticks"* conventional approach also happens to be the way that most companies structure their reward and recognition systems. The research Pink cites proves exactly the opposite, especially for individuals doing work that involves more than manual tasks. He makes the distinction between extrinsic motivations (from sources external to us such as money or prizes) and intrinsic motivations (those internal to us as people). He argues for the latter, not the former in the context of the Twenty-first century.

This extrinsic-intrinsic distinction is not new. It has been identified and studied by psychologists for decades, principally in the work of Abraham Maslow and Frederick Herzberg. But Pink provides a modern landscape, adds recent research and layers in the historical context and company practices. He further distills his analysis into three elements which are easy to understand and resonate with existing research on engagement and commitment. His three intrinsic elements are:

- **Autonomy:** Being able to make your own choices in terms of task, time, technique and team. The opposite of autonomy is having decisions made for you, even if you might agree with them.

- **Mastery:** The desire to get better and better at something that matters. The highest, most satisfying experiences in people's lives are when they are in *"flow."*

- **Purpose:** To be associated with something important. *"The most deeply motivated people—not to mention those who are most productive and satisfied—hitch their desires to a cause larger than themselves"* (Pink, 2009).

How do these findings contribute to HR as a decision science? How do they make better use of talent? A pragmatic answer came from a leading pharmaceutical company in Canada. The CEO challenged the company leaders to reverse engineer autonomy, mastery and purpose into their workplace. As a result of taking these actions, significant engagement and productivity results have been demonstrated.

b. The 70/20/10 Development Framework

> *"The only real security that a person will have in the world is a reserve of knowledge, skills and ability."*
>
> *Henry Ford*

For decades, the practice of employee development was thought to be synonymous with training. If you needed new skills, you enrolled in a training course. You left work to learn something new. This view was partially perpetuated by a multi-billion dollar training industry, but it never seemed to be quite accurate. Most of us know that we learn from doing, sharing, and reflecting on our own activities and experiences.

The Center for Creative Leadership (CCL) thought differently about development. In the 1980s Morgan McCall, Robert Eichinger and Michael Lombardo proposed the 70/20/10 Learning and Development Framework that included learning from work experiences and connecting with others (Figure 5). While the initial self-report research that led to the 70/20/10 percentages is more suggestive than definitive, the labeling has stuck and many organizations have embraced this more inclusive developmental framework.

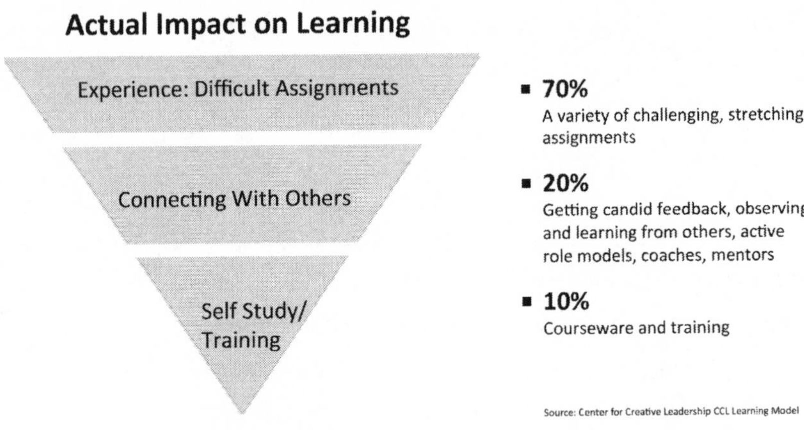

Figure 3-7: The 70/20/10 Learning and Development Framework

This 70-20-10 framework is being used to make decisions about the most efficient and effective ways to develop talent. It views the workplace as the primary learning laboratory, not the classroom. It is ironic that the majority of corporate learning budgets goes to the 10% (formal training programs) that, according to the 70/20/10 model, often has the least impact on learning.

c. The 9-Box Leadership Development Framework

The 9-Box Framework is a widely used tool to calibrate future leaders in an organization and identify their next developmental experience. Although the 9-Box framework is used to make decisions about people, it should be used primarily as a developmental tool.

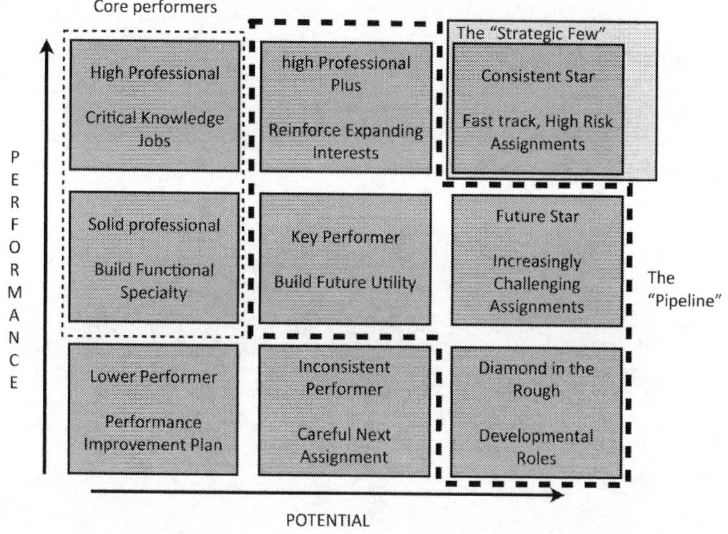

Figure 3-8: The 9-Box Leadership Development Framework (Korn Ferry, 2012)

The 9-Box Framework is a decision tool for making the best choices for future leaders. It is not, however, an exact science. But the 9-Box still qualifies as a decision support tool because it:

- Details a structure to the process.
- Provides opportunity for specific definitions of performance and potential.
- Enables evidence to be examined that impacts future development options.
- Builds on the consensus of next level managers, not a single person's opinion.
- Creates a consensus among the management team.

8. Improving the Workforce and Workplace: The Engagement, Collaboration and Retention (ECR) and Bersin Models

A key role of strategic HR is to create the context in which talent can flourish and be the architect of an improved workforce and workplace. When this happens, HR becomes a *"force-multiplier"* that improves business outcomes and transforms organizations. Several decades of research have provided guidance on how to achieve these goals. There are two encompassing models—based on this research—that should influence decisions about the environment and context within which talent operates.

a. The HCI Engagement, Collaboration and Retention (ECR) Framework (HCI, 2011).

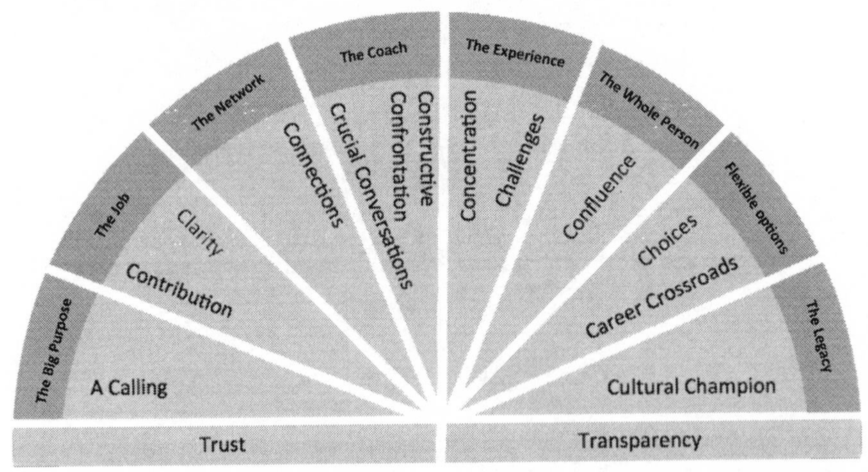

Figure 3-9. The HCI Engagement, Collaboration and Retention (ECR) Framework

The ECR Framework was developed in 2011 and refined in 2014. The Framework is comprised of 2Ts and 13Cs, and it provides a blueprint for HR professionals to create the environment in which talent, productivity and innovation can flourish. It defines the characteristics of a successful workplace, both for individuals and organizations. The components of the ECR Framework are as follows:

- **The Foundation Built on Trust and Transparency.** These qualities are essential to any partnership and reciprocal relationship between the employee and employer. Key thought leaders: Stephen Covey, Tony Hsieh, Dov Seidman.
- **The Big Purpose (A Calling):** The importance of belonging to an organization pursuing worthwhile goals. Organizations that support the triple bottom line: profits, people and principles. Key thought leaders: Dan Pink, Chip Conley, Simon Sinek.

- **The Job (Clarity and Contribution):** A line of sight between a job and its contributions to company goals. The clearer this internal alignment, the more engaged and committed the employee. Key thought leaders: Marcus Buckingham and Leigh Branham.
- **The Network (Connections and Community):** Creating communities within larger organizations where people feel valued and involved. We are all community builders now. As Gary Hamel has said *"Communities outperform bureaucracies every day of the week."* Key thought leaders: Gary Hamel, Reid Hoffman, Seth Godin.
- **The Coach (Crucial Conversations and Constructive Confrontation):** Having trusted advisors who can provide honest advice, open conversations and meaningful feedback. These coaches create a cycle of value. Key thought leaders: Marcus Buckingham and Marshall Goldsmith.
- **The Experiences (Concentration and Challenges):** Continuing to grow and develop skills and experiences. At the end of the day, the greatest security and mobility we have is continuing to develop our own capabilities. It is often more about career than job security. Key thought leaders: Dorothy Leonard, Noel Tichy, Mark Murphy.
- **The Whole Person (Confluence**): Focusing on all aspects of a person, not just at work. The boundaries between work and life are now illusory as we are always connected to work; but personal well-being needs to be respected and protected. Key thought leaders: Tony Schwartz, Dave Ulrich, Ken Blanchard.
- **Flexible Options (Choices and Career Crossroads):** Providing options, flexibility and choices so that employees create their own context. This becomes an *"opt-in"* organization. Key thought leaders: Gary Hamel, Cathy Benko, Ram Charan.
- **The Legacy (Cultural Champion):** Creating a culture of sustainable values that guide the organization through turbulent times. Moving to the desired and not the default culture. Key thought leaders: Rosabeth Moss Kanter, Dov Seidman, Tony Hsieh.

b. The Bersin Framework (2014)

The Bersin Framework is entitled *The Simply Irresistible Organization* (2014) and it identifies five major elements and 20 different characteristics. This framework shares many of the characteristics in the Great Places to Work research and in the Goffee and Jones Harvard article entitled *"Creating the Best Workplace on Earth."* (HBR, 2013) The Simply Irresistible Organization Framework is as follows:

Meaningful Work	Great Management	Fantastic Environment	Growth Opportunity	Trust in Leadership
Autonomy	Agile Goal Setting	Flexible, Humane Environment	Facilitated Talent Mobility	Mission and Purpose
Selection to Fit	Coaching and Feedback	Recognition-rich Culture	Career Growth in Many Paths	Investment in People; Trust
Small Teams	Leadership Development	Open, Flexible Work Spaces	Self and Formal Development	Transparency and Communication
Time for Slack	Modernized Performance Management	Inclusive, Diverse Culture	High-impact Learning Culture	Inspiration

Figure 3-10: The Simply Irresistible Organization Framework (Bersin, 2014)

9. Building Compelling Cases for Change

HR professionals must not only be able to use methodologies and tools to make the best decisions about talent, but they need to argue for the value that these programs and solutions provide. Organizations only have so much energy, and there will always be competing priorities for resources. HR professionals need, then, to argue persuasively for their projects and initiatives; and there are guidelines that can assist in developing compelling cases for change. Consider the Model for Compelling Cases for Change presented by Condit and Forman (2012).

Case for Change	The Justification is:	Likely Prospects
The Alignment Case	The linkage to strategy, strategic initiatives and business goals. Risk: Working on the wrong problem.	Chief Executive Officer Direct reports to CEO Key Variable: More likely if major strategy change is being implemented or a new direction is needed.
The Business Case	The capital investment provides a better return than other options. Hurdle rate and payback period are very positive. Risk: Not making the best investment.	Chief Financial Officer Finance staff Leaders with strong financial orientation Key Variable: Focus depends on current financial strength.
The Experiential Case	The qualitative and emotional improvement in the workforce, workplace, culture and marketplace. Risk: This subjective result does not impact the business.	Customer-facing leaders Service-oriented businesses Strong social media presence Key Variable: For businesses trying to recover/strengthen credibility, brand strength and employee engagement.
The Comparative Case	Scores or ratings among key competitors. Using benchmarks to *"see how we stand."* Risk: A backward looking analysis that tells little about the future.	Executive Team Leaders who compete against these competitors every day. Key Variable: The pecking order of competitors; some are more important than others.
The Null Case	The risk of doing nothing. This is a rhetorical argument that challenges inaction. Risk: Upsetting leadership	CEO Executive Team Key Variable: The propensity of the executive team to act.
The Continual Case	Making cases often to key stakeholders. Once is not enough. Risk: Keep the messages varied and interesting.	Sponsors, Stakeholders Key Audiences Key Variable: Message overload in a busy company.

Figure 3-11. Compelling Cases for Change (Condit and Forman, 2012)

These, then, are a sampling of nine methods and models that are available to HR professionals. Some of the presented models have been developed by HR, while others have origins in finance, strategic planning and consulting practices. Some models are more descriptive than predictive, but all help to organize information, facilitate decision making and optimize the use of talent, money and other scarce resources.

Recommendations and Insights:

1. More than Enough Models

The Human Resources profession has a myriad of models, frameworks and methodologies that influence the use and effectiveness of talent in an organization. The models presented in this chapter run the gamut from encompassing frameworks that improve the workforce and workplace; to alignment models that link talent to strategy; to human capital value chains; to financial tools to justify HR expenditures. There are doubtlessly many more frameworks that could have been presented, but the point is that the HR models that exist provide structure and guidance in making better decisions about people.

2. Mindsets Matter

If HR believes that it is a soft discipline, then it will be a soft discipline. The reality is that HR has a robust set of models at our disposal. HR needs to know what these various models are, and then be confident in their use. We should be able to explain their rationale and derivation to business leaders so that they can share confidence in their use.

HR, for example, tends to think that its models are not as robust as those in the Finance function. But if you talk to finance professionals, it becomes clear that financial statements are based on projections, not fact. Revenue and profits are projections of what people think will happen, not absolutes. These projections can change quickly as a new order drops out, a sudden expense is discovered or receivables take longer to collect. Berman and Knight (2013) reveal that accounting and finance are as much art as science:

"The art of accounting and finance is the art of using limited data to come as close as possible to an accurate description of how well a company is performing."

HR has a strong set of models and methodologies. But there are always gray areas, assumptions and subjectivity in any function, no matter how precise they may seem.

3. **Speak the (Understandable) Language of the Business**

   Boudreau provides solid advice when he advocates using business tools and models, because presumably business leaders are already familiar with them. The overall goal is to weave talent and strategic HR practices into businesses processes so there is no distinction at all. It becomes natural to discuss strategy and business direction in the same conversation about the talent needed to achieve these goals.

   Even when using existing business tools, it is important to consider the business leaders being influenced. There can be a downside to methodologies and tools if they are too esoteric. Some concepts such as *return on improved performance (ROIP)* may be comfortable for one executive while it could be obscure for another. Esoteric models, even if used by some part of the business, may not be persuasive to all. It is more important to determine the outcomes that are important to the business and use common-sense models and frameworks that can be clearly understood and communicated to many constituencies.

4. **It's About Execution**

   As we have seen, HR has a robust set of models and methods. A greater level of HR success comes not from different or more models and methodologies, but with a confidence and the ability to implement the ones we have. As Stephen Covey has said: We don't need more intelligence in organizations (IQ), we need more XQ—the execution quotient. Instead of worrying about more or better tools, let's worry more about being the drivers of change, executing well, speaking persuasively and improving the business with the models and methodologies we have at our disposal.

TOOLS AND TEMPLATES

Six tools are presented that have been derived from the HR methodologies, models and frameworks previously discussed.

Tool 1: Strategic Workforce Planning: Segmenting Roles

A basic tenant of Strategic Workforce Planning is the segmentation of roles that provide the most value to the organization. This practice is similar to customer segmentation, but applied to the workforce. The four workforce role segments are strategic, core, supporting and misaligned. The advantage of role segmentation is that it enables focus on the roles that provide the most value. Development resources, for example, should be funneled more to strategic and core roles, and succession plans should be developed for these roles as well. Add the specific roles for your organization in the third column and gain consensus with business unit leaders.

Segment	Description	Roles
Strategic	Necessary to achieve strategic goals and future success About 10 to 15% of roles	
Core	Operational excellence. The engine of the enterprise that is core to delivering products and services About 20 to 25% of roles	
Supporting	Internal operations work efficiently; supporting core and strategic roles About 60 to 70% of roles	
Misaligned	Jobs that no longer provide value; employees can be redeployed. Goal is 0% of roles	

Tool 2: Fitting Top Talent to the Most Valuable Roles

It certainly makes sense to have the organization's best people working in the most crucial jobs. This fit makes perfect sense to business leaders and executives. According to Becker, Huselid and Beatty (2010) many organizations segment their talent by potential and performance. Fewer organizations segment their roles, and even fewer attempt to align their top talent to the most valuable roles. Complete this tool for your division or group.

The value of this tool can also be demonstrated by considering the outliers and mismatches between the highest and lowest categories.

- If C Level talent is working in Strategic Roles, the organization is likely at risk.
- If A Level talent is working in Support roles, there is a high likelihood that the best performers will become disengaged and leave the organization.

	A Talent	B Talent	C Talent
Strategic Roles			
Core Roles			
Supporting Roles			

Tool 3: Optimizing the Fit between Store Managers and Revenue Potential

This simple tool had a significant impact on a major retailer. It improved revenue and profit by 25 to 30%. It is based on the simple question: Are the best managers in stores with the greatest revenue potential? In some cases there may be intentional reasons for excellent managers to be placed in other stores, but in general, great managers led to great financial results. This company found that mid-level managers restricted the growth of the highest performing stores. This tool is similar to Tool 2 in which talent levels are matched to different roles. Both Tool 2 and 3 are examples of optimizing talent deployment.

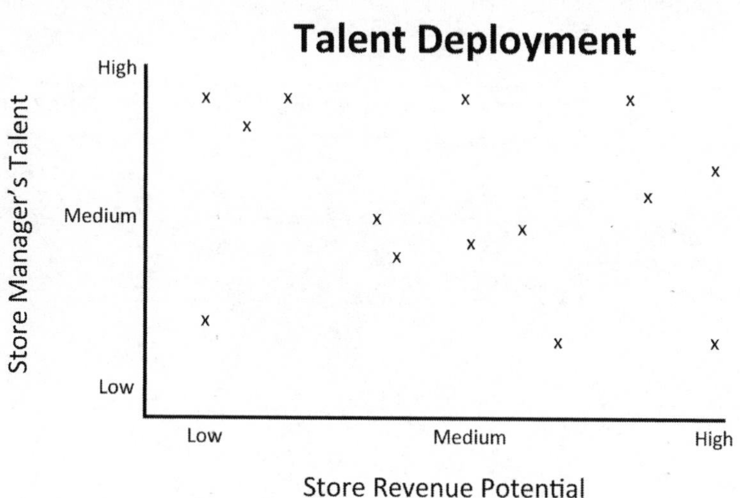

Tool 4: The 70/20/10 Learning and Development Portfolio

Given the 70-20-10 Learning and Development Framework, it is a relatively simple matter to create development portfolios based on important competencies to the organization. These can be created once and then provided to managers so that they can work directly with employees to make the best selections for inclusion into their ILPs (Individual Learning Plans). It can be difficult for managers to create these portfolios themselves, so it is useful to give them resources they can work from.

Notice that this portfolio does not have the percentages of 70/20/10 because there may be more or less entries based on the situation. Also, there is an emphasis on learning from *new* experiences, not all experiences. Not much learning occurs if people are performing similar tasks over and over again.

Competencies	**Learning from New Experiences**	**Learning from Others**	**Learning from Courses, Materials and Interventions**

Tool 5: The ECR Model: Stay Interview

Many organizations are revamping performance management systems in favor of more regular conversations between managers and employees. Atlassian Software, for example, has 12 monthly conversations a year instead of perhaps one or two. The Stay Interview is a simple but effective tool to help implement this plan. These common-sense questions demonstrate an interest by the manager and they yield information that can be acted upon. Not all of these questions need to be asked each month; but it is important that regular touchpoints and conversations continue to occur.

Questions	Responses
What do you enjoy most about your work?	
Are there some aspects of your job that you would like to change or improve?	
What do you see as your top three strengths? Are you utilizing them in your work?	
What do you need to get better at and how might this impact your performance?	
How can I help you improve and achieve your career goals?	
Is there any reason why this may not be the right place for you?	
Do you have any suggestions for me?	

Tool 6: The Cost of Unwanted Turnover

The costs of unwanted and unavoidable turnover can be significant, especially in certain industries. The general figure for the cost of losing people you don't want to lose is 1.5X their fully burdened salary (Ulrich, Boudreau, HCI). This is a valuable guideline, but it is also useful to calculate this figure for key positions and people. Cisco, for example, knows that every time it loses and engineer it costs the organization $250,000. One HR Leader calculated the cost of losing people in strategic roles and presented these figures to the Board as a way to justify developmental programs for these roles. These investments were quickly approved

The Cost of Losing Good People	Financial Impact
1. Total Hiring Costs: For one job, X number of candidates are needed	
Recruitment fees	
Advertising fees	
Staff costs to review profile and make selection	
Screening time for X candidates	
Background checks for X candidates	
Assessments and testing for X candidates	
Interviews for X candidates	
Administrative time for X candidates	
Travel costs to meet X candidates	
Relocation fees	
Sign on bonus	
Administrative costs to make arrangements for new employee	

2. Total Severance Costs	
Severance fee and services	
Outplacement fees	
Costs in negotiating separation	
Exit Interview costs	
Unemployment insurance premiums	
3. Lost Productivity Before and During Vacancy	
Reduced productivity while employee considers leaving*	
Time the position is vacant**	
Reduced productivity of co-workers	
4. Declining Productivity While On-boarding New Employee	
Time of the on-boarding period	
Productivity learning curve costs***	
Manager's cost	
Training costs	
5. Other Ramifications—Harder to Quantify	
Lost training and developmental investment	
Lost knowledge and skills	
Lost relationships contacts, and customers	
Declining workforce engagement and morale	
Missed opportunities****	

* Exiting employee productivity is 75% or less while considering leaving.

** Use 50% of fully burdened salary for lost productivity for the amount of time the position is vacant, even if colleagues are sharing the work.

*** Different jobs have different times to 100% proficiency. In general: 25% productive from weeks 1 through 4; 50% from weeks 5 through 12; and 75% from weeks 13 through 20.

**** Used especially for sales positions. This number can be very large

SUMMARY

HR is more of a decision science than we know. While we tend to think that other disciplines have better tools and methods, it is perhaps that they have done a better job marketing their tools than HR has. This chapter has presented a number of tools and models, some of which are HR-generated while others have other derivations. All of them can be used to make better decisions about the workforce and workplace so that costs are saved and productivity is enhanced.

There is nothing wrong with our toolset. It continues to evolve and grow all the time. It might be nice to be able to be as precise as an engineering lean process improvement practice. But our practices involve people and work, often within a constantly changing and turbulent environment. By definition, this is more subjective because that is the reality of the modern workplace. So while our models may be more descriptive and sequential than *"fool proof,"* they still provide guidance, direction and leverage to make better decisions about talent, alignment and business outcomes.

Chapter 4

Perception Four: HR Measures are Too Soft and Subjective

> *"In the New Economy, human capital is the foundation of value creation. This presents an interesting dilemma: The asset that is most important is the least understood, the least prone to measurement and the least understood."*
>
> *David Norton*

David Norton wrote those words more than a decade ago as a way to introduce the *Balanced Scorecard Model* that provides leading indicators in addition to the traditional financial measures of a company's performance. The Balanced Scorecard was also one of the first tools to integrate both financial and non-financial information to create a more balanced and complete view of the organization.

It is important to acknowledge that some things are easier to measure than others. It is easy to measure the presence or absence of physical items. We built 15 ladders on Tuesday. Our cash reserves are $59 million. It is easy to measure activities that did or did not occur. The training class was held on

Friday and 23 people attended. There were 24 new hires last month. But are these types of HR measures meaningful or insightful?

> *"Just because something can be counted, doesn't mean that it counts."*
>
> *Albert Einstein*

There are two other factors that influence the belief that HR does not have adequate measures. The first is the comparative view that HR measures are not as solid as, for example, Finance. Accounting and Finance, with its 500 year history, have standards such as GAAP (Generally Accepted Accounting Practices) and reports such as Balance Sheets and Income Statements that are consistently used in business and industry. Finance is nice, neat and orderly; or is it?

As we have seen and as financial professionals know, finance is anything but neat, orderly and objective. Assumptions and biases are just as much part of financial statements as are $ signs. In reality financial measures, especially when processes such as revenue recognition, profit projections and accruals are considered, can be much more subjective and complex than HR measures.

The second factor contributing to the belief that HR measures are not substantive is that HR databases and systems are often fragmented and rarely integrated. Bersin (2014) states that HR data are often in 7 different systems in the enterprise. It is true that different data sets on employees, job candidates, learning and development activities, talent pools, engagement and employee surveys are difficult to integrate. But this picture is changing as HR systems are becoming more powerful and prevalent. Even without perfectly synchronized data, there are many improvements that can be made by using analytics that are close at hand.

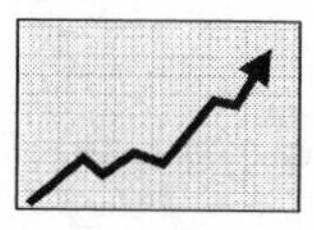

THE EVIDENCE

Is HR measuring just what is easy, safe and convenient to measure? Can HR measures lead to business improvements? Let's examine the evidence and examples to see if HR measures are being used to make better business decisions.

Analytics in Other Disciplines

The marketing profession has been using analytics for decades. These analytics, along with the practice of segmenting market audiences, has led to messaging that has improved customer satisfaction, loyalties and revenues. All customers are not the same, as some have unique needs and have more buying power. This understanding and use of marketing analytics has become a competitive advantage for the organizations that do it well. These same principles used to analyze customers outside the organization can be used *internally for employees.*

The use of analytics to make more informed decisions is not limited to marketing. Pease, Byerly and Fitz-enz (2013) have identified other industries that have long-used analytics to improve their operations and profitability, including:

- Financial Services: Credit scoring, underwriting and fraud detection
- Retail: Inventory replacement and demand forecasting
- Transportation: Scheduling and yield optimization
- Manufacturing: Supply chain optimization and yield optimization

Davenport and Harris (2007, 2010) have written extensively on the value of analytics and use in different industries. While the power of analytics has come lately to HR, relatively speaking, its value is not in question.

> *"Future organizational performance is inextricably linked to the capabilities and motivations of a company's people. Organizations that have used data to gain human capital insights already have a hard-to-duplicate competitive advantage."*
>
> *Davenport and Harris, 2010*

Two Reasons for Using Human Capital Analytics

It is important to be clear about the reasons that time, resources and energy are spent to gather and analyze data. It can be easy to fall in love with the process and forget the purpose. In general, data and analytics should enable better decisions to be made, but this statement is often too general to be meaningful. Two more specific reasons for gathering and analyzing data are to :

1. **Determine successful talent practices so that they can be replicated.** Modern organizations are laboratories for different practices and activities. Some of these initiatives are more successful than others, and it makes sense to try to replicate the successful practices again and again. This provides leverage, enables the organization to learn from itself and builds on proven practices. For example, if leadership development programs prove to be more effective when leaders teach leaders, then this practice should be institutionalized across the organization.

2. **Uncover potential risks to the organization and take actions to mitigate them.** This purpose is especially important for Boards of Directors and CEOs. They are trained to identify risks and address them before they progress to be problems. A number of potential human capital risks can uncovered by examining analytics, including poor leadership pipeline, significant retirement eligibility; imbalanced workforce; outdated skillsets and excessive turnover.

Two Types of Inquiries

There are two ways in which HR can use analytics to make better decisions about leveraging positive practices and mitigating potential risks. The first way is to work with business unit leaders to address their business priorities, strategic initiatives and requests. This approach can be labeled the inductive approach. An example of an inductive inquiry would be if a CEO feels uneasy about high turnover among younger employees and asks HR to examine the problem.

The second approach is to get into the data and see what patterns emerge. This is more of a deductive approach, in which the HR professional plays the role of detective. A detective is always looking for clues, traces and relationships, and this mining of the data can yield surprising, unanticipated insights. The insights from deductive analyses often yield responses of *"I didn't know that"* or even *"wow."* An example of a deductive finding was when Intuit discovered that engineers who stayed with a manager for more than 3 years had more limited career opportunities. This finding was a complete surprise to Intuit management.

The two types of inquiries complement each other and both are needed. In one case, inductive inquiries support stakeholders and business strategy and goals. In the other, deductive analysis uses the workplace as a laboratory in which findings may emerge and hypotheses can be tested.

Moving From Measuring HR Efficiency to Effectiveness to Impact

HR, like many functions, has tended to count what is easy and convenient to measure. It is easy to measure the number of hours employees spend in training, or the number of open requisitions, or the satisfaction scores for training courses. This information may be interesting to some, but not to business leaders. Boudreau and Ramstad (2007) have made the distinction among efficiency, effectiveness and impact measures. HR has historically focused the most on measuring activities and efficiency, while business leaders are more interested in effectiveness and especially impact.

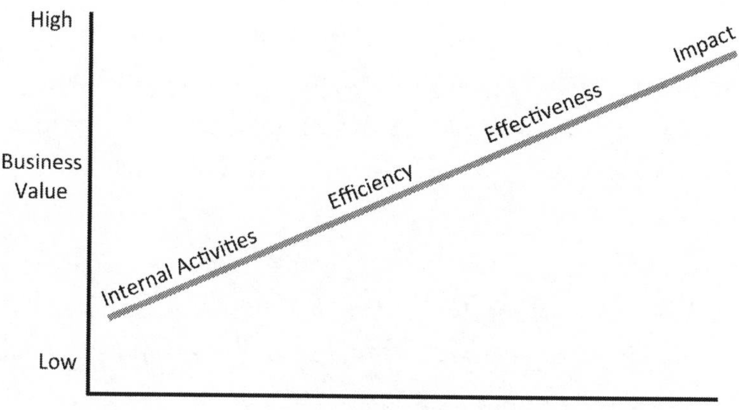

Figure 4-1: The Business Value of Different Human Capital Measures

A case in point is recruiting metrics. The two most popular recruiting measures are time to hire and cost to hire. These are relatively easy to measure, but as efficiency measures, they say nothing about the quality of the job done by the new hires or the impact they have on the organization. A recruiting organization can be very efficient at bringing in all the wrong people into the organization. A more valid recruiting quality measure is Quality of Hire (QoH) because it addresses effectiveness and impact.

Use of Human Capital Analytics

A 2015 report by the Harvard Business Review Analytic Services is encouragingly entitled: *"HR Joins the Analytics Revolution."* HR is not yet a fully-fledged partner; and by some estimates it will take a decade to fully join the party. After all, according to an SAP/HCI study (2014), 43% of organizations are still using spreadsheets or other manual reporting methods. But the direction has been clearly established. The HBR study notes that 57% of companies expect to be using data integrated across various systems within 2 years. This is clearly a target for the $15 billion HR software market.

In terms of current patterns for using data to make workforce decisions, the following is reported.

- **11%:** We rarely use data to inform workforce decisions.
- **40%:** We use data reactively—typically via ad hoc reporting—to inform only critical workforce decisions.
- **26%:** We use data proactively—typically via operational reporting.
- **15%:** We analyze our workforce proactively—typically via dashboards and visuals that are up to date and available on demand.
- **9%:** We analyze and make proactive predictions about our workforce—typically via dashboards and visuals that contain predictive analytics.

> *"We have seen a sea change in the last 12 to 18 months. We see CEOs and others wanting better data and not just a head count report, but how talent is driving business results. There is clearly movement to more integrated data, on-demand access and predictive analytics that can help "manage tomorrow, today."*
>
> *Scott Pollack, PwC Saratoga 2015*

The SAP/HCI research provides additional insight. It segments analytics users based on their technical and analytical capabilities.

Category	Distribution	Characteristics
Pioneers	16%	Strong in both technology and analysis skills. Strong in defining roles properly, predicting talent needs and aligning the workforce. High customer satisfaction.
Analysts	10%	Strong analytical skills, but little technical infrastructure. Strong correlation to defining roles properly, predicting talent needs, and aligning the workforce. Data not available to others.
Technologists	41%	Relatively strong technology infrastructure, but weaker analytical skills. Not correlated to defining roles properly, predicting talent needs, and aligning the workforce. Data are widely available.
Beginners	33%	Just getting started. Less likely to measure what is important. Not related to defining roles properly, predicting talent needs and aligning the workforce.

Figure 4-2: SAP/HCI Research on Human Capital Analytics (2010)

This research shows that HR is in the early stages of using human capital analytics for making better talent decisions. There are twice as many beginners as pioneers. It is also interesting to observe that analysts' skills are in short supply, and this is much more of a limiting factor than the technology itself. As in many problems, technology may be seen as the solution; but in reality it takes informed people to use the information wisely and make change happen.

Company-Specific Examples

Specific companies, using their own data, have used analytics to make better decisions about the workforce and workplace. As previously mentioned, these decisions either 1) leverage successful practices or 2) minimize a risk that has been identified. The following examples have been taken largely from the work of Thomas Davenport, Lauri Bassi, Laszlo Boch and HCI.

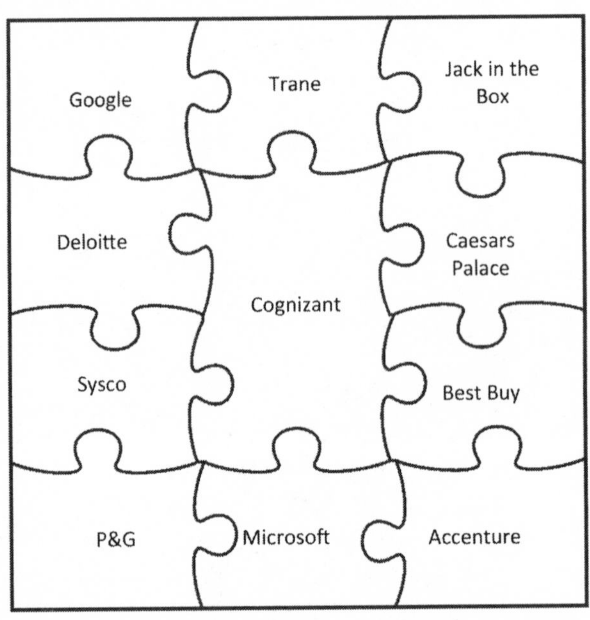

Figure 4-3: Companies Using Human Capital Analytics to Make Better Business Decisions

1. Google on Effective Managers. Project Oxygen was created to study the question of the value of people managers at Google. In a technical company such as Google, the role of manager is often not appreciated; and perhaps the company should have project managers instead of people managers. A research study—Project Oxygen—was undertaken to determine if people managers mattered and should be retained. This study has been documented in the New York Times, a Harvard Business Review article and a chapter in Laszlo Boch's *"Work Roles (2015)"*.

Project Oxygen compared manager ratings from performance reviews (top down view) and employee surveys (bottom up perspective), and determined that effective people managers did matter. Then the study tried to determine the qualities of effective managers. They derived eight qualities, and then took systematic action to weave these characteristics into talent practices and the culture of Google. The eight characteristics that were identified:

- Be a good coach
- Don't micromanage
- Express interest in team member's success and well being
- Be productive and results oriented
- Be a good communicator and listen to the team
- Help employees with career development
- Have a clear vision and strategy for the team
- Have technical skills so that you can advise the team

While this list may not be surprising, these are some interesting findings. First, the characteristics are listed in order of importance with being a good coach at the top of the list. Second, many believed that technical skills would be more important than some of the *"softer"* manager qualities. And third, while many of these characteristics may be *"common sense,"* they were not clearly common practice. Google, therefore, took great strides to incorporate these characteristics into training, recognition and development programs as well as into ongoing surveys and analytics.

2. Google on Optimum Number of Interviews: Even with the envious record of receiving over 2 million resumes per year because of its great reputation, Google had become famous for its torturous hiring process. It hired *"great people at a snail's pace."* The hiring process could take six months or longer, and a candidate had to endure up to 25 interviews before an offer was extended. Each hire took up to 250 hours of employee time, and candidates who did not get offers were not particularly complimentary of the process.

As Google grew, it examined its hiring practices just as it would its customer-facing products and services. Laszlo Boch (2015), the head of People Operations for Google, described this investigation.

"We constantly review and work to balance our speed, error rate and quality of experience for candidates and Googlers. One team member looked at the question of whether having up to 25 interviews per candidate was actually helpful or not. He found that four interviews were enough to predict whether or not we should hire someone with 86% confidence. Every additional interviewer after the fourth added only 1 percent more predictive power. So we implemented a "Rule of Four" and redesigned our hiring process. This shaved our median time to hire to 47 days and saved employees hundreds of thousands of hours."

Laszlo Boch, 2015

3. Microsoft and P&G on Quality of Hire: What is the best source of new talent for an organization? Quality of hire (QoH) is a critical measure for talent acquisition, and as previously discussed, it is an effectiveness (not efficiency) measure. QoH is usually operationalized to mean: do new hires do a good job, do they stay with the company and do they become high performers over time?

Microsoft examined QoH for new hires and discovered that Waterloo University, in a suburb of Toronto, produced truly outstanding application developers who often went on to be among the highest performers. One reason for this excellence--in addition to a distinguished faculty—is that students are expected to work in teams, on tough technical projects, with changing requirements, and have to make frequent reports to leaders/executives. These are exactly the conditions that will be faced in a job at Microsoft. Given this type or preparation, it is hardly surprising that Microsoft considers Waterloo graduates to have the equivalent of five years of professional experience upon graduating.

Proctor and Gamble (P&G) also examined quality of hire for incoming MBA graduates. In an organization built on its brands and people, these positions are crucial for future growth. P&G found that MBAs from excellent Mid-western Universities had the highest QoH. It wasn't because MBAs from Stanford and the Ivy League were not smart enough, it is just that they tended to change jobs faster than the company desired. If people change jobs every two to three years, they are probably not in position long enough to impact results.

4. Best Buy on Store Engagement: Is there a relationship between engagement and financial performance? By examining the relationship between engagement levels and revenue at the store level, it was determined that a .1% improvement in store-level engagement is related to $100,000 in increased revenues. This finding underscored the value of concentrating on store-level engagement programs.

5. Jack-in-the-Box on Engagement and Alignment: Jack-in-the-Box fast-food restaurants followed a similar research design to correlate restaurant-level engagement, capabilities and alignment with financial, customer and business performance. The findings: Restaurants with more engaged and aligned employees have 21% less turnover, 5% higher guest satisfaction, 10% higher sales (revenue), and 30% higher profits.

6. Sysco and Trane on Impacts of Engagement: Unlike, Best Buy and Jack-in-the-Box, these two companies are not in the retail sector; and they sought to determine if there were business and financial benefits to strong human capital practices and an engaged workforce. For Sysco, a major trucking and transportation company, its operating units with highly satisfied employees had lower costs, reduced turnover, higher customer satisfaction and higher revenues. For Trane, an equipment manufacturing and sales organization, higher human capital practices led to improved safety in plants and stronger sales results in sales offices.

7. Deloitte on the Monetary Impact of Unwanted Turnover: This major accounting and consultancy firm wanted to investigate the costs of unwanted turnover. Unwanted turnover is especially important for Deloitte as its talent is its primary product. The finding is that a 1% drop in unwanted turnover equates to a savings to the firm of $400 million. This is obviously a huge number, and it would seem to justify most investments needed to keep talented partners in the firm.

8. Caesars Palace on Healthcare Benefits: Caesars wanted to explore the benefits and costs of its wellness and health programs. There is a cost to the company for these programs, but a research team found three significant, measurable benefits. People who participated demonstrated: 1) reduced absenteeism, 2) higher levels of employee health and engagement, and 3) an increase in preventative care visits with corresponding reductions in significant health procedures....saving millions of dollars.

9. Cognizant on the Value of Bloggers: This information technology consulting company wanted to investigate what impact, if any, participation in social media had on business performance. This is a timely topic, with many organizations having policies pertaining to social media usage at work. Its findings are that bloggers, in particular, are more engaged and are 10% more productive than employees in general. One possible hypothesis for this result is that bloggers care so much about what they are doing that they take time to reflect and write about it. This finding would certainly argue for continuing and expanding opportunities for people to express themselves via social media channels.

10. Accenture on the Value of Training: Accenture took a longitudinal view to determine the characteristics that lead to successful consulting projects. In this case, success means: the engagement was completed on time, on budget and with high customer satisfaction ratings. The data show that a key factor in successful projects is the extent to which project team members are updated and trained on the skills needed on the project. This finding, while probably not surprising, is so much more impactful than standard measures of training such as number of people trained or percentage of payroll applied to employee development.

These examples of company-specific uses of analytics are by no means exhaustive. There are many, many other examples that are revealed all the time in the works of Thomas Davenport, Jac Fitz-enz, Laurie Bassi, Ed Lawler to name just a few; and in publications such as The Harvard Business Review, The Sloan Management Review, Talent Management, Chief Learning Officer and HR Magazine. While some of this research may be more robust than others, the consistency of the results is compelling: Talent analytics are being used by companies to make better decisions about extending success and mitigating risks.

Recommendations and Insights:

1. Human Capital Analytics Work Just Fine

As we have seen, there are many examples of human capital analytics leading to better business results. There is nothing wrong with HR metrics; they are not too soft or subjective. They may not be as precise as, for example, the types of manufacturing tolerances from six sigma projects, but that is beside the point. HR data are the foundation for 1) driving business results by creating the context in which talent and innovation can flourish; 2) improving business results through better alignment, cost savings and productivity improvements; and 3) becoming a trusted and respected business leader.

HR as a profession needs to become more data-driven and evidenced-based; and we have the tools, measures and examples to make this happen. As HR technology continues to advance, the access to the data and its subsequent use in improving the business should only increase.

2. The Commitment to Take Action

There should be an unspoken principle that accompanies the effort and resources it takes to analyze workforce data: It is not enough to gather data and find patterns, it must lead to action. This principle gets back to the ultimate purpose for analyzing metrics in the first place; it should yield intelligence to make better decisions regarding leveraging success and/or mitigating risk.

The case in point for the commitment to take action is Google's Project Oxygen. While this study answered important questions and led to valuable findings, its real impact came as the findings were incorporated into ongoing processes and the culture of Google. This is where Project Oxygen made a difference to the organization.

3. **Focus on the Consequential Few**

It is easy to get overcome with data. To some extent this is natural, especially as a more deductive approach to data gathering is used. In this situation, you mine through a lot of data to find the truly meaningful relationships; but then you focus on these critical few as opposed to the inconsequential many. Data paralysis can easily happen if you look at too much data. It's too confusing, there is too much to do, and the really important opportunities get lost.

It is also easy to become enamored of all that is being measured, regardless of its importance to measure. One senior HR leader talked about this phenomenon when she said: *"We measure what we value, not value what we measure."*

A good rule of thumb followed in many talent scorecards is to monitor about 5 to 7 measures at any one time. This number coincides with the capacity of short term memory to process information (which is often placed at 7 items, plus or minus 2). This guideline keeps the analytics process manageable, and again emphasizes the importance of prioritization.

4. **Don't Let Perfect be the Enemy of the Good**

As big data comes to HR, there will be greater sophistication in human capital analytics. This is inevitable and welcomed; but it can also lead to ignoring findings that are simple and small. Small data can be as powerful and meaningful as big data. Do not fall into the trap that attaches value only to advanced studies that employ sophisticated statistical techniques. For example, there are ways to conduct interviews and focus groups to gain insight that can improve the business right now.

Tools and Templates

Tool 1: 2x2 Matrix Example

This is an example of a relatively simple use of metrics. It does not use sophisticated statistics and analytical techniques. It simply presents two fields of data and then looks for the linkages that exist. The various positions within a company are placed in the quadrants based on their impact and retirement eligibility. The implications from this example are clear; there are some positions that require immediate action by recruiters and developers to mitigate the risk of a workforce without the required capabilities and experiences

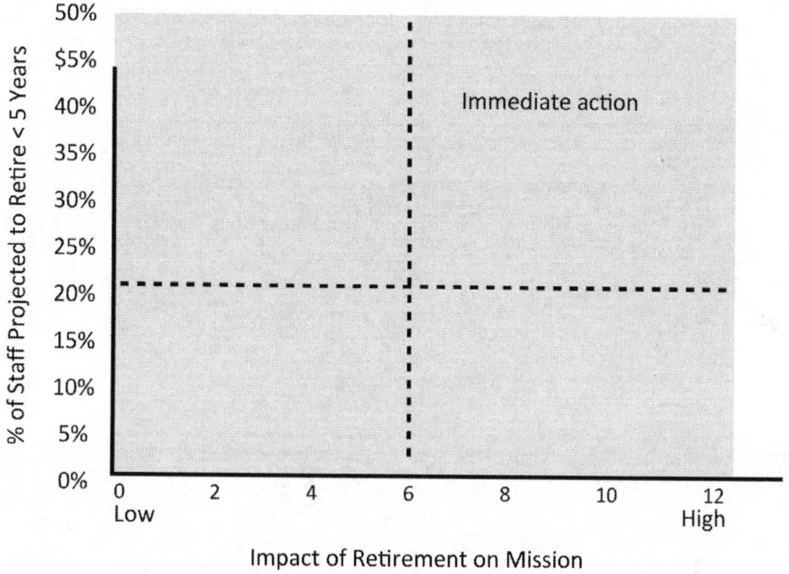

Figure 4-4: Retirement Eligibility for Critical and Strategic Roles

Tool 2: The Measurement Map

Pease, Byerly and Fitz-enz (2013) have created a practical tool that links initiatives to strategy on the one hand, and leading indicators to business results on the other. The linkage between strategy and the initiative is important because it shows that the initiative furthers the implementation of strategy. The linkage between leading indicators and business results is significant because it focuses the initiative on achieving business results. This tool also addresses the issue raided by Boudreau and Ramstad that HR has been unduly focused on measuring efficiency, not effectiveness or impact. Complete this tool for key initiatives or projects.

Strategy	Initiative	Leading Indicators	Business Results

Tool 3: Workplace Vulnerabilities (Forman, 2014)

This tool is based on a presentation at HCI's 2014 Workforce Planning and Analytics conference on measures associated with potential workforce risks. It should be noted that while these measures pertain across industries and companies, they may not be the most meaningful for a particular company. This list must therefore be evaluated separately for each organization to determine its relevance.

Measure	**Rating of Importance** (1 not important to 5 very important)
Engagement and turnover by location, function, demographics, tenure and manager	
Engagement levels of top performers and high potentials	
Depth of leadership and strategic role pipelines	
Retirement eligibility by role, location and expertise	
The optimum balance of build/buy for new leaders and build/buy/borrow for narrowing skill gaps	
Diversity levels throughout the organization	
Time to proficiency, especially for strategic jobs	
Number of high potentials and top performers in strategic roles	
Quality of hire and candidate experience	
Internal talent mobility fill rates	
Company collaboration participation rates	

Tool 4: Meaningful Outcome Measures

Each organization must determine the business outcome measures that are most critical to monitor on a regular basis. Also refer to the outcome measure tool in Chapter 2 that links outcome measures to specific business leaders.

Outcomes	Specific Measures	Importance (1 not important to 5 very important)
Innovation	Number of new products Number of new patents Sales from new products	
Quality	Rework rate Wastage Expert and customer reviews	
Productivity	Revenue per employee Output per employee Industry benchmarks	
Customer Loyalty and Satisfaction	Net promoter score % of repeat business Customer surveys	
Time to Proficiency	Productivity measures Peer ratings Manager ratings	
Competitive Differentiation	Expand strengths Improve weaknesses Market share gains	
Strategic Accomplishment	Meets objectives Exceeds objectives	
Cost Savings	Reduce costs through eliminating tasks Reduce costs through more efficient processes	
Efficiency	Reduce time to task Reduce hand-off times	
Effectiveness	Quality of development programs Quality of hire	
Revenue	Increased revenue Increases by product, market segment and service area	
Profit	Increased profit Increases by product, market segment and service area	

Tool 5: Appreciative Inquiry Questions

HR professionals are often asked to be consultants to investigate potential problems, implement change and execute organizational strategy. Data and evidence play a significant role in these investigations. A technique used by consultants for this type of organizational inquiry is *"appreciative inquiry"* which means find what works and try to replicate it. This technique focuses on strengths and successes, not weaknesses or failures.

Heath and Heath (2010) offer similar advice in their book *Switch: How to Change Things when Change is Hard."* They suggest *"following the bright spots"* because these people and projects have figured out success. In spite of difficult situations, perhaps a reluctant culture and limited resources; there are always positive spheres of success. According to this line of inquiry, you can learn a lot more by studying success than trying to discern failure.

Focus	Sample Questions	Finding
Manufacturing Plants	Why are some plants more productive than others? What are the key process differences between our most productive plants and others? What characterizes the work environment in the plants with the best safety records?	
Sales	Why are some sales offices more successful than others? What are the characteristics of the best sales reps and managers?	
Different Company Locations, or Groups	Do we have locations or offices that can serve as models for other locations? Why do some locations have higher engagement scores than others?	
Managers	What attributes distinguish our most successful managers from others? What are the characteristics of managers with the highest employee loyalty?	

SUMMARY

While HR may not yet be a fully evidence-based profession, the intention and movement is apparent. In the Global Human Capital Trends, 2015, Deloitte research says that while 75% of firms state that using people analytics is important, only 8% of organizations rate their abilities as strong. And the HCI/SAP research previously cited indicates that the barrier may be less about technology than the analytical skills of HR professionals. There is progress to be made, but the direction is clear.

There are two fundamental purposes for using analytics: 1) find out what works and replicate it, and 2) identify possible risks before they become problems. These two goals contribute to HR being a *"force multiplier"* (spread success) and *"a lead time ahead"* by proactively identifying risks. Analytics, then, are not a nice to do activity, but fundamental to HR accomplishing its three impacts: 1) create the context in which talent and innovation flourish, 2) improve business results through better alignment, cost savings and productivity improvements, and 3) become a trusted and effective business leader. Data-driven HR is paramount to driving business results.

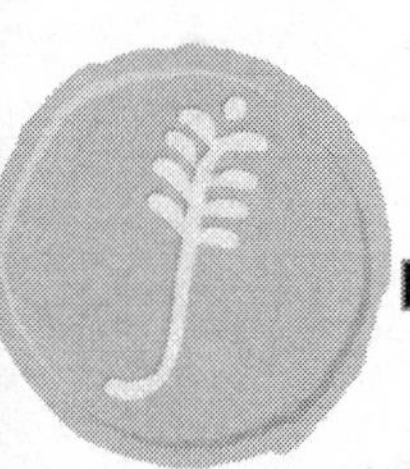

Chapter 5

Perception Five: HR is a Stodgy Dead-end Career

> *Let's face it, the HR profession is not held in the highest regard…My diagnosis, in part, is that the profession doesn't have the right mix of talent in it, which creates a vicious cycle where the most talented people, who want to work with other talented people, shy away from the field.*
>
> *Laszlo Boch, 2015*

It can be entertaining to read articles that cast aspersions on such well-worn topics as taxes, politics, FIFA, the banking laws…..and HR. Almost everyone has an opinion and something to say, at least in private. Two articles have definitely left their mark on the HR profession and how it is regarded. The first is not so well known but very colorful, while the second was a blockbuster and is still being discussed a decade after its publication.

In 1981, Professor Wickham Skinner of the Harvard Business School penned an article entitled *"Managing Human Resources."* It was not a complimentary view, and he invoked the Texas descriptor of *Big Hat, No Cattle* to imply that the HR profession was all promise and no action. There was no there, *there* according to Skinner. He observed that businesses had spent millions trying to make employees loyal, motivated and productive, and all to little or no avail. It must be remembered that the time frame was 1981. The economy was shifting more to services but many company practices were still anchored in the industrial era. Global competitors were outperforming the US: Productivity was down, faddish movements were in, economic prospects were not promising and public confidence was wavering. So for the time, Skinner was right: HR had not demonstrated the ability to add value and contribute to business results. And the phrase he used resonated with his audience, *"Big Hat, No Cattle,"* is now part of the history and lexicon of HR.

A decade and half later, Keith Hammonds challenged the HR profession. *"Why We Hate HR"* was published by Fast Company in 2005. It was a dialectic aimed at getting discussions and conversations going, and it worked. Part of Hammond's success is that his observations rang at least partly true. His stated reasons to hate HR:

1. HR people aren't the sharpest tacks in the box. HR is not attracting top talent, doesn't speak the language of the business and is often a resting pace for people who have not succeeded in other roles.

2. HR pursues efficiency in lieu of value. HR measures activities and internal practices, not outcomes or results.

3. HR isn't working for you. HR pursues standardization and uniformity; its *"one size fits all"* approach is easier to implement, but seriously undermines the top performers who drive innovation and business results.

4. The corner office doesn't get HR. There is a serious disconnect between CEOs and what they expect and get from Human Resources.

SHRM, to its credit, not only acknowledged the article after its publication in 2005, but published a Teaching Guide (2006) to facilitate discussion among its members. Since the article appeared, there have been ezine articles entitled *"Why we still hate HR"* but none of these has had the impact and influence of the Hammond's original.

Just like the engaging phrase *"Big Hat, No Cattle,"* part of the appeal of Hammond's article is the title. It's catchy and has staying power. It would be a mistake, however, to think that this belief does not still exist. For example, in 2015, Kyle Smith in Forbes has written *"It's Time for Companies to Fire Their HR Departments."* The reasons he cites for HR's failings are familiar:

- They speak gibberish
- They revel in red tape
- They live in a bubble
- They aren't really in your business

There is another contributing factor to the perception that HR is a poor career choice. George Bernard Shaw, in his play *Man and Superman,* had one of his characters utter the phrase: *Those who can, do; and those who cannot, teach.* Shaw's sentiment has also been used to characterize HR professionals who really can't do much else but be in HR.

Other professions suffer from outright bias and demeaning stereotypes as well. There are geeks in IT, nerds in finance and empty suits in sales. Where would we be today without great geeks and inventive nerds? HR just seems to have more than its fair share of derisive labels that do little to address issues or lead to lasting improvements.

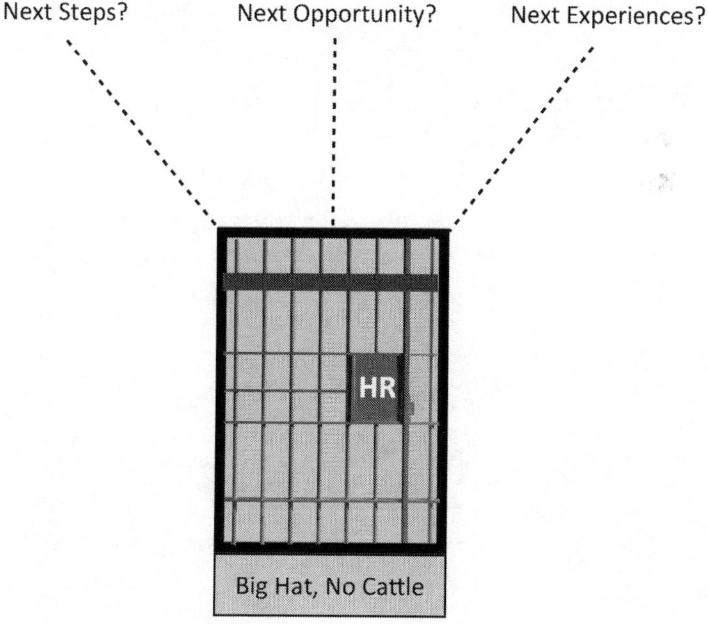

Figure 5-1: A Dead-End Career

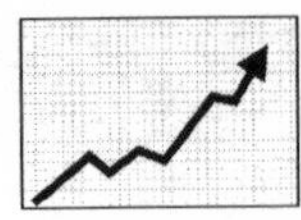

The Evidence

The perception that HR is a dead-end destination exists today, but is this true? Is this belief less or more prevalent now than when Skinner and Hammonds expressed their views? Is HR a more lively and relevant career choice today for high performers? Is HR preparing leaders for loftier roles? Is HR offering exciting new challenges or simply replicating the past? It turns out that there is interesting evidence to consider.

1. ***"Why We Chose to Go into** HR."* In August of 2008, two Harvard MBA graduate students published this article in the Harvard Business Review. Matthew Breitfelder and Daisy Wademan Dowling talked about their choice to pursue HR as a profession. Their journey is treated in some depth because it offers such a stark contrast to the impression that HR is a lackluster endeavor.

> *"A career in human resources isn't the typical destination of a Harvard MBA. We're supposed to be employed as strategy consultants or investment bankers, or in the true spirit of the degree, general managers. We once had those jobs, but we don't now, and we know what our classmates are thinking: "It's a work/life balance thing." They don't have the stomach for 'real business.' If you can't do, teach. And of course our favorite: 'If they're so interested in helping people, why don't they just go into social work. Well the answer is simple, and we relish providing it.* HR *today sits smack-dab in the middle of the most compelling competitive battleground in business, where companies deploy and fight over the most valuable of resources—workplace talent."*
>
> *Breitfelder and Dowling, 2008*

They acknowledge HR's shortcomings [*administriviators*], the fact that CEOs often say one thing and do another, and the reality that many traditional HR activities are being outsourced; but they continue to see the opportunity for bright, dedicated HR professionals to make a significant impact on the business.

> *"As talent management becomes a make-or-break corporate competency, the HR function is responding with a shift from managing the monetary levels of human resources—compensation, benefits and other expenses—to increasing the asset value of human capital, as measured by intangibles such as employee engagement. A new kind of HR professional is emerging to manage this transformed function."*
>
> *Breitfelder and Dowling, 2008*

It is interesting to hear them reflect on their training as MBAs and how this impacted their career journey. They discuss HR in the language of the smart investor and portfolio manager.

> *"In business school, we were trained to seek out underappreciated investment opportunities and to create value in surprising places. Unlike our peers searching for bargains in private equity or at hedge funds, though, we see the deepest discounts in the complex task of identifying, attracting, developing and deploying people. We also see an undervalued and underappreciated asset in the HR function itself, one that is poised to appreciate significantly. Like the smart value investors we learned to be in business school, we wanted to get in early."*
>
> *Breitfelder and Dowling, 2008*

Finally, Breitfelder and Dowling discuss what the new face of HR looks like. They have specified five important characteristics.

- **It Looks Like a Business School.** The focus becomes solving real-world business problems with teams of people working together using their analytical skills and learning from each other. The teams use their functional expertise to add different perspectives and insights, beyond what a single department could offer.

- **It has a P, Not Just an L.** Forward-looking companies treat HR as an engine for both savings and revenue, deliberately blurring the lines between business activity and people development. Usually HR is associated with just cost reductions, but the role of improving productivity and the *"top line"* can be significantly greater.

- **It Hatches and Harvests Ideas.** *"Ironically HR, long perceived to lack innovation, can become both the catalyst and facilitator of mechanisms that foster creativity across organizational boundaries."* Ground-up innovation programs become the *"secret sauce"* for organizations that compete in the Innovation Age.

- **It Makes Big Places Smaller.** Gary Hamel has said that *"communities outperform bureaucracies every day of the week,"* and HR is perfectly positioned to establish meaningful connections and communities across the enterprise. HR becomes the connective tissue of the organization.

- **It Focuses on the Upside.** It is essential to address critical problems, but greater benefit can often be achieved by maximizing strengths, focusing on the upside, and leveraging what already is successful. In organizational psychology this approach is called *"Appreciative Inquiry"* as it leverages and builds on the positive. (See Chapter 4, Tool 5)

What a great list! While this article is more of a personal expression than a scientific study, it does represent a very different view of HR than the prevailing myths that HR is a dead-end. Let's examine more evidence and data points.

2. Laszlo Boch at Google: "Work Rules (2015)." This book is a first-hand account of the people practices at Google, from the person who should know. Laszlo Boch is the Senior Vice President of People Operations at Google (the top HR job), and his story is an interesting one.

Born in Communist Romania, Laszlo did a variety of things as a young man including working in a library, a restaurant and doing a walk-on for Baywatch. After more experiences, he got his MBA and was hired by McKinsey to work with technology firms. Several years later he was frustrated as he observed that business plans fell apart when not supported by people and that while CEOs always spoke of people first…they treated them like *"replaceable gears."* As Boch thought about his experiences, he determined that his next step would be to find a way to influence how entire companies treated people. He decided to find a job in HR.

His colleagues at McKinsey thought he was delusional and committing professional suicide. But Boch, true to his vision, knew otherwise.

> *"At the time, there were more than five thousand people in the McKinsey database of alumni, but only a hundred of them were in human resources, virtually all working as consultants for other firms or recruiters. I reasoned that my training and background would make me stand out in the HR talent pool and help me come up with novel solutions. And maybe, just maybe, that would help me have a faster career trajectory than waiting twenty or thirty years to creep up the corporate ladder. I might get to a place where I could impact more people, faster.*
>
> *Laszlo Boch, 2015*

It seems to have worked out OK as Google has been named the Best Place to Work for an unprecedented five times in the United States and similarly recognized around the world. According to LinkedIn, Google is the most sought after place to work anywhere, and every year over 2 million resumes are sent to Google hoping for a vaunted employment slot. Reflecting on his experience at Google, Boch offers his perspective.

> *"Far from professional suicide, my time at Google has been a white-water ride of experimentation and creation. Sometimes exhausting, sometimes frustrating, but always surging forward to create an environment of purpose, freedom and creativity."*
>
> *Laszlo Boch, 2015*

This again is a meaningful personal story with many similarities to Breitfelder and Dowlings' journey. The primary difference between these two personal cases is that Google's culture and people practices speak for themselves and have impacted thousands of people; while *"Why We Chose to Go Into HR"* is more about promise, opportunity and aspiration.

3. HR at GE and P&G: The Academy Companies. There are several dozen companies that have demonstrated exemplary people practices for decades. Typically, these *academy companies* had legendary CEOs who almost intuitively understood that people practices were the key to their success and longevity. While their peers were laboring in the vestiges of Industrial Age practices, this new breed of CEOs were creating competitive advantage by reframing the picture. They included such notables as Sam Walton, Jack Welch, Larry Bossidy, Andy Grove, Wayne Calloway, Herb Kelleher, Fred Smith and A.G. Lafley.

It is interesting to observe that even with these sterling examples of CEOs who believe that a company can *only succeed in the marketplace after being successful in the workplace,* it has taken many years for this belief to become mainstream. It is just further evidence that old perceptions die hard and that it can take decades for new views to become accepted and embraced.

From this pantheon of legendary CEOs there are two stories that need to be told. The first is a Jack Welch story from *"Winning (2005)"* and his time at GE. One of his primary management tenets at GE was to "*elevate HR to a position of power and primacy in the organization and make sure HR people have special qualities to help managers build leaders and careers.*" He was giving a presentation on his management views and was asked about the role of HR within a company. Without hesitation, Welch responded:

> *"Without doubt, the head of HR should be the second most important person in the organization. From the point of view of the CEO, the head of HR should be at least equal to the CFO…After all, if you managed a baseball team, would you listen more closely to the team accountant or director of player personnel. The input of the team accountant matters—he or she knows how much to pay a player. But this input certainly doesn't count more than input from the director of player personnel who knows just how good each player is."*
>
> *Jack Welch, 2005*

The second story is about P&G, another great academy company. During A.G. Lafley's first stint as CEO, a new headquarters office building was being designed, and the key question was: *"where should all the executive offices be placed?"* The executive committee decided to do a time-in-motion study to gather data on communication patterns among executives so that the offices could reflect this organic pattern. All the executives agreed, at least until the results of the study were revealed.

Lafley called a meeting to address the situation. The recommendations were that the two closest offices to the CEOs were the Chief Marketing and Chief Human Resources Officers. The heads of major business lines (with multi-billions in sales) were on the floor but slightly removed from the CEOs office. These slightly displaced executives were not thrilled, as the story goes; but Lafley responded that, first, they all had agreed to a process and would live with the results even if not to their liking. And second, Lafley said that he agreed with the recommendation because, at the end of the day, P&G is about its *brands and its people.* Enough said. The meeting proceeded in an orderly fashion from then on.

4. Why HR Chiefs Make Great CEOs—Really! This article appeared in the December 2014 issue of the Harvard Business Review. It began with the impressions of Ellie Filler, a senior partner with Korn Ferry (executive recruiting firm), who specializes in placing senior HR executives. She had noticed a major shift in the requirements for the job, moving from administration to being the CEO's key advisor. She believes that this role is gaining importance like never before….it is now becoming much more of a game changer as the CHRO makes presentations to the Board and is a key person in implementing strategy.

While Filler's insights are valuable, she wanted to go beyond her impressions. She partnered with Dave Ulrich to examine data relevant to the new CHRO role. Their findings and recommendations follow.

- In examining the pay of top performing executives, the top three on the list are: CEOs, COOs and (surprisingly) CHROs. The average top decile performing CHRO's salary is $574,000, which is 33% more than Chief Marketing Officers.

- They then examined 14 leadership attributes grouped into three categories of leadership style, thinking style and emotional competency.

They reviewed executive team members to see who more closely approximated the CEOs skill sets. The finding was that with the exception of COOs (whose responsibilities often overlap with the CEOs), the closest skill set match was with CHROs. As Dave Ulrich said, *"This finding is very counterintuitive—nobody would have predicted it."*

- Based on these findings, the authors' recommendation: More companies should consider CHROs when looking to fill the CEO position.

Filler and Ulrich argue that potential CEOs spend developmental assignments in top HR jobs. They believe that the best CEO candidates are executives with broad operational and managerial experience ***that includes*** HR leadership assignments. The authors cite two examples of CEOs who had significant developmental stints with HR earlier in their careers. Mary Barra of GM and Anne Mulcahy, previously of Xerox, both attach great importance to their time in HR, and how it prepared them to lead their respective companies.

> *"It is almost impossible to achieve sustainable success without an outstanding CHRO. The CHRO should be a sparring partner for a CEO on topics like talent development, team composition and managing culture."*
>
> *Thomas Ebeling, former CEO of Novartis*

5. HR ***Growth and the*** HR ***Job Market.*** The sizing of the HR job market is certainly an indicator of a profession on the rise or decline. There are currently over 90 countries that have HR associations committed to improving the skills and abilities of HR professionals. A quick perusal of the largest job boards is a good data point. But the rub comes from a more basic question: what constitutes an HR professional? Is it someone with HR in their title (easy answer, but incomplete)? Or is it someone who provides HR services (regardless of their title) within a company? Or is it someone in the HR consulting industry that provides services to client organizations. Or is it all of the above?

The numbers can scale quite quickly if the more inclusive definitions are taken. For example, LinkedIn counts over 2 million people who list their jobs as working in HR. This is considerably larger than, for example, the membership of the Society for Human Resource Management (250,000 members). The Bureau of Labor Statistics goes above and beyond. It says the number is more like 4.4 million people demonstrating at least some HR capabilities in 2012.

Job category	Sizing (2012)	Comments
Human Resource Managers	102,700	Does not include some of the newer titles like people operations.
HR Specialists	495,500	Includes internal and external recruiters.
HR Analysts and Consultants	718,000	Is inflated because it includes management consultants who may not be focused on HR.
Training and Development Managers	28,600	Probably a good estimate.
Training and Development Specialists	228,800	Probably a good estimate.
Compensation and Benefits Managers	20,700	Probably a good estimate.
Compensation, Benefits and Job Analysis Specialists	91,700	Probably a good estimate.
Occupation and Health Specialists	58.200	This sometimes resides within HR and sometimes not.
Payroll Auditors	1,275,400	Probably highly inflated as most are in the domain of finance.
Employment and HR Clerks	1,404,000	Inflated because it includes the job of information clerk.

Figure 5-2: Bureau of Labor Statistics HR Job Listings (2012)

These data may or may not be enlightening as there are clearly categorization issues at such a high level. It is also important to remember that these estimates are for the United States only (the domain of the Bureau of Labor Statistics). What is clear is that a great many people are HR professionals demonstrating their skills everyday in the marketplace.

Another indicator of a vibrant profession is the forecast for future growth within an industry segment. Monster, Indeed and the Bureau of Labor

Statistics all indicate that HR (in numbers of people and jobs) is growing faster than the average for all jobs. The growth percentages are double digits, ranging from 12% to 15.5% to as high as 21%. It is also interesting to observe that HR Budgets are increasing at a 4% rate, even with the cost and efficiency pressures to do more with less (Bersin, 2015).

"The CNN Money website ranks HR manager as the fourth in its list of best jobs in the United States, based on the high level of flexibility and creativity, and manageable levels of difficulty and stress. It's an important and growing field. The Bureau of Labor Statistics predicts a significantly higher than average growth rate for HR jobs in the entry and specialist levels between 2010 and 2020." Mary Bauer, Demand Media, 2015

A final indicator of the strength of a profession can be gleaned from examining the external market, in this case for HR consulting and technology services. The talent management software market alone is now a $5 billion dollar market growing at 17%. The more fully-featured Enterprise Resource Planning (ERP) systems market, which contain HR and other functional capabilities, is five times as large. The global Human Resources Outsourcing market is massive, with some estimates approaching almost $200B by 2017 (Companies and Markets.com, 2015). The markets for these various products and services are growing, some faster than others; but the direction and trending have all been positive.

*6. **Respected Thought Leaders.*** A stodgy profession has little intellectual activity. It is boring, dull and repetitive. It doesn't spark much debate, controversy or change. It isn't disrupting itself. Is HR a boring, stodgy profession?

One indicator is to look at published articles and books in a defined period of time. The Harvard Business Review (HBR) is a respected journal that is read by over 265,000 people, including many business leaders. During the course of a year, there are roughly 70 featured articles published in HBR, and at least one-third of these articles pertain to new management ideas, leadership, innovation, organizational change and leveraging talent—all of which pertain to the role that HR can play in organizations. Many of these HBR articles have been used as source materials for *Fearless HR*. There are a variety of other valued journals and magazines with new articles and research that impact

HR, from both the HR industry itself and general business/strategy field. And the proliferation of web sites and blogs has been nothing short of algorithmic.

It is also useful to review the list of the most influential business consultants and strategic thinkers to see which ones contribute to HR topics and priorities, either directly or indirectly. There are a variety of lists of the most influential management thinkers, and there is usually considerable agreement among the consultants rated. Forbes has reported on the Thinkers50 ranking with the following consultants at the top of the list.

- Clayton Christensen
- W Chan Kim and Renee Mauborgne
- Roger Martin
- Dan Tapscott
- Vijay Govindarajan
- Rita McGrath
- Michael Porter
- Linda Hill
- Herminia Ibarra
- Marshall Goldsmith
- Pankaj Ghemawat
- Jim Collins
- Daniel Pink
- Lynda Gratton
- Amy Edmondson

This is obviously a partial list, but virtually all of these thinkers impact organizations, how they innovate and execute strategy, and therefore HR's role as architect of the workforce and workplace. These thought leaders and others such as Gary Hamel, Marcus Buckingham, John Kotter and Dave Ulrich, not only influence, but impact HR in its mission to become a trusted and capable business leader.

7. "It's Time to Split HR." Ram Charan is a highly respected management consultant, thought leader, and author. His article *"It's Time to Split HR"* in the

July-August, 2014 HBR issue has focused more attention to the best organizational structure for HR. CEOs tell him they want HR to be more strategic.

They (CEOs) would like to be able to use their chief human resource officers (CHROs) the way they use their CFOs—as sounding boards and trusted partners—and rely on their skills in linking people and numbers to diagnose weaknesses and strengths in the organization, find the right fit between employees and jobs, and advise on the talent implications of the company's strategy.

But Charan believes that the current HR structure mitigates against this likelihood. He proposes an HR-A group that reports to the CFO and focuses on administration, benefits and compensation. He then proposes an HR-LO (leadership and organization), reporting to the CEO and focusing on improving the people capabilities of the business. Furthermore, he espouses that HR-LO be led by operational, marketing/ sales or finance leaders whose business expertise and people skills give them a chance to attain the top two levels of the organization. In this manner, the top HR jobs become developmental assignments and not a ticket-punching exercise. This stance is very similar to the previously espoused views of Filler and Ulrich.

There are two other prominent examples of splitting HR into strategic and operational groups. The first is the United States Government. In 2002, the Chief Human Capital Officer (CHCO) Act was enacted as part of the Homeland Security Act. It required 24 government agencies and departments to appoint a Chief Human Capital Officer whose job would be to modernize HR, revamp HR policies, project future talent needs, and improve the ability to hire, engage, develop and retain employees. This act also established the CHCO Council to encourage collaboration and common approaches among the 24 CHCOs. HR Departments continue to exist, but they focus on operational and transactional activities. HR and CHCOs serve side by side in the government, each with different purposes and roles.

The second example is Cisco Systems and the fact that they did what Ram Charan suggests, two years before he wrote his article. Cisco split HR into tactical and strategic wings with the latter focusing on such initiatives as strategic workforce planning, career plans and assigning metrics aligned to overall business strategy. General Business Services (GBS) focuses on operations of both HR and IT shared services, with a strong emphasis of efficiency and quality employee experience. The latter is essential so that employee experience is improved while also decreasing costs. Don McLaughlin, Vice President of Employee Experience at Cisco, discussed the logic of this separation.

> *"For a number of years, there has been a notion of getting HR to become a more strategic partner to the business, to really understand talent management, workforce planning and organizational design, to fully comprehend where the business is heading and how to make it grow. But the business always wants immediate help in the transaction space, The tyranny of the urgent draws resources into day-to-day work, and it creates a struggle of ever getting to the higher level of work."*
>
> *Don McLaughlin, 2013*

Dave Ulrich comments on this separation of the tactical and strategic: *"Both create value, but tactical issues have to be managed to drive efficiency while strategic issues are managed to create innovation. The logic, thinking, tools and activities for the tactical and strategic ideas are different, so they should be managed and worked through differently."*

The organizational debate will go on, and there is no single best answer: Context, history and, most of all, talent matter. But this is not a discussion about HR being a stodgy career, not adding value or antiquated. Rather it is a discussion about how to optimize the value that HR is capable of providing.

The perception that HR is a dead-end job continues to persist, but the evidence tells a very different story. Whether the evidence is personal testimony, research, job growth or CHRO career paths, there is clearly a lot of activity, movement and even momentum in the HR profession today. Just look around: Every week there is new information to assimilate, understand and apply. The profession is on the move.

Recommendations and Insights:

1. A Great Opportunity to Shine

Boch, Breitfelder and Dowling all saw the great opportunity for HR. There are certainly problems to address, but the vision espoused by Jack Welch and A.G. Lafley is obtainable with the right HR talent, capabilities and mindset. The opportunities abound and as Laszlo Boch has said, there is an advantage for first movers. It is probably true that because of the perceptions that have plagued the HR profession (and thereby restricting the flow of talent), there is more opportunity for people in this field who have the passion, belief and skills to succeed. The window of HR opportunity, however, will not exist indefinitely. Seize it.

2. Get HR Out of Its Shadow: Improve Visibility and Credibility

HR is terrible at marketing itself. Perhaps this is because of a belief that marketing really isn't necessary. Nothing could be further from the truth, especially when trying to change perceptions that have handicapped the profession for years. HR needs to promote itself, shine the spotlight on results, and get aggressive.

- *Increasing Visibility.* Visibility is about being seen, having an active presence and leaving silos. It's about getting out and getting together. It's about being perceived as a *"happening group"* and creating a vibe. Some possible actions: One-on-one check in meetings monthly (see the Stay Interview tool); presenting at town halls; orchestrating on-boarding sessions; sponsoring community events and wellness initiatives; bringing in speakers and providing learning experiences; initiating best picture/cultural story contests; introducing an HR learning week; working in cross-functional teams; bringing fun into the workplace; and driving engagement survey actions.

- *Improving Credibility.* Credibility is not just about doing things, but doing important things. It's about adding value that matters, solving tough problems, and making bona fide improvements. It's about impressing the people that are the formal and informal leaders of the organization. Some possible actions: Coaching leaders; making presentations to the Board; piloting ground-up innovation programs, using analytics to anticipate potential future risks; creating initiatives to build and shape the desired culture; anticipating future workforce capabilities; and building options, choices, and transparency into the workplace.

3. Mindsets Matter

Self-fulfilling prophecies can be a curse or a blessing. The problem with HR is we tend to the negative and therefore the *"curse"* side of the equation. Humans, in general, are wired to be more questioning and critical because it is our survival instinct. We need to determine pretty quickly if its fight or flight. However, negative emotions narrow people's vision according to Barbara Fredrickson, the leading researcher on positivity. Furthermore, Rozin and Royzman have found that negative perceptions are more contagious than positive views. Negative experiences are stored in our brains much faster than positive ones, and in general, it takes 5 to 10 positive events to counterbalance one negative event (Williams, 2014). So a positive mindset takes work. It is somewhat against our natural instincts, but a positive perspective is essential if HR is to overcome the myths and negative impressions of the past

4. Don't Stop Moving

There are lessons to learn from Facebook. One of their core values is *"Move fast and break things."* Perhaps *we could forget the breaking part*, but the essence is true. The defining characteristic of organizations today is the unrelenting change that they face. The market- facing sides of organizations must change and adapt; but the internal groups are often under no such immediate pressure. The result is that these internal groups (such as HR) become outdated and use processes that were developed for the past. HR, even as it ascends to being a business leader, force multiplier and architect, must continue to change and adapt just as fast as the business itself.

Tools and Templates

The purpose of these tools and templates is to broaden HR's perspective, promote a clear alignment between the business and HR, and improve the marketing effectiveness of HR.

Tool 1: Executive Perceptions of HR

There may be a variety of different perceptions and expectations for HR within the executive team. It is valuable to know these perspectives and be able to adjust actions accordingly. This is a good exercise for the HR team to complete, and then update as conditions change over time.

Executive	Perception of HR	Expectations for HR	Communication Plan

Tool 2: Building Visibility: HR Participation in Cross-Functional Teams

This tool helps to track the visibility of HR into the organization by its participation in cross-functional teams. This is important, not only to make sure HR's voice is heard, but also for HR professionals to learn from their colleagues. See the discussion on tacit knowledge in Part II of *Fearless HR*. This is also an excellent way to continue to grow one's professional network.

HR Professional	Cross Functional Teams	Key contacts

Tool 3: HR Developmental Positions

As Ram Charan suggests, because HR touches the people of the organization, it is an excellent assignment for high potential future leaders. These leaders may be from operations, finance and other parts of the organization, or from HR itself; but it is useful to plan these types of assignments. It is also important to begin to think about future candidates from throughout the organization. In this tool, identify which jobs in HR could be developmental assignments for people from other groups. Once identified, note the current occupant of the job, the probably length of tenure, and likely next candidates.

Developmental Position	Current Occupant	Length of Assignment	Next Probable Candidates

Tool 4: Building HR Visibility and Credibility

HR needs to be better at marketing itself. The two key tasks are to increase visibility (being seen, having an active presence, and breaking down barriers) and improve credibility (adding value to the business and improving business outcomes). It is important to build intentional campaigns for both visibility and credibility because negative perceptions about HR will not change by themselves. This is a great activity for the HR team: first to brainstorm possible actions and then to commit to implementing the ones that can make a difference.

	Actions	**Campaign Theme**	**Time Frame**
Building Visibility	1. 2. 3. 4. 5. 6. 7.		
Building Credibility	1. 2. 3. 4. 5. 6. 7.		

Tool 5: Favorite HR Resources

It can be difficult to keep up with the proliferation of research and best practices in the field of HR. It grows by leaps and bounds almost daily. Since one duty of a professional is to keep abreast of his or her field, this tool can be a useful aid. It ideally should be user-generated content that is developed by the HR team itself.

Articles	Books	Authors/ Consultant	Blogs	Websites	Discussion Groups

SUMMARY

Hardly *"Big Hat, No Cattle!"* It's not 1981 anymore, and we know so much more about the value that HR can and has provided. Old opinions die hard, but when you hear the personal stories of bright MBA students, CEOs of the academy companies and the Head of People Operations at the Best Place to Work in the world, they present a different picture, full of challenging opportunities.

There truly is an advantage for early movers to *Fearless HR*. There is an advantage personally as Laszlo Boch can attest, and there is an organizational advantage to embracing a model that has proved to be so effective.

It is a fascinating time to be an HR professional; so much is on the line. There are certainly tough problems to address and fix. There continues to be disappointment from CEOs about HR's ability to lead and impact business results; and these issues must be addressed. But there is nothing inherently wrong with the profession, it is not forever flawed, nor doomed to second class corporate citizenship. The perceptions that have dogged HR in the past, are just that: myths that are contradicted by evidence, experience and leadership. It is time to leave these errant beliefs behind and move to solutions that can address the real problems that organizations face today.

> *"It is time for HR to make the same leap that the finance function made in recent decades and become a true partner to the CEO. Just as the CFO helps the CEO lead the business by raising and allocating financial resources, the CHRO should help the CEO by building and assigning talent, especially key people and working to unleash the organization's energy."*
>
> *Charan, Barton and Carey, 2015*

Part 2

The Opportunities

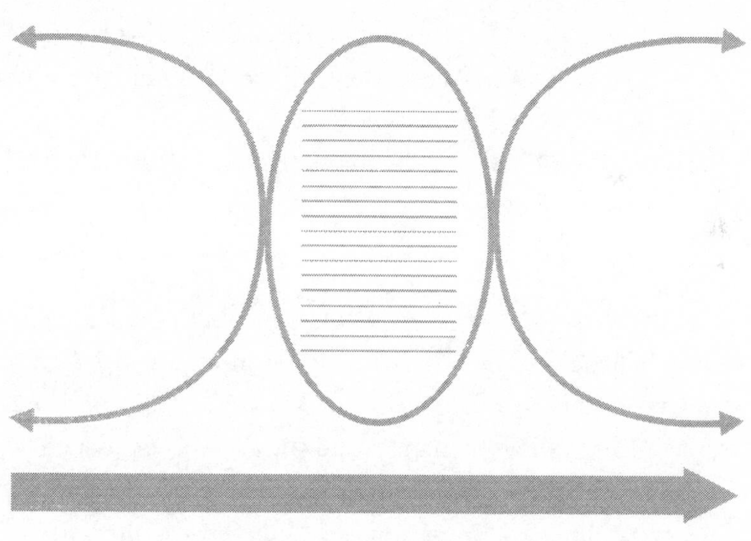

The elephants in the room have been addressed. The pachyderms, just like the perceptions that have surrounded the HR profession were clearly there, but rarely confronted. As a result, the myths continue to influence actions, just as Mark Twain said they would in 1882. In his humorous story of *The Stolen White Elephant,* inept detectives fail to find this largest of animals right in front of them. But let's not make the mistake that debunking myths means that everything is rosy for HR. It is not and serious challenges remain, just as they would for any profession seeking to add value in this uncertain, turbulent business environment.

The picture from research is equally challenging. In *Global Human Capital Trends 2015,* various authors from Deloitte make the following observations:

- The capability gap for HR is growing. There is a gap between how HR leaders perceive themselves and how business leaders view HR's performance. The former is higher than the latter.
- The question is, do HR organizations have the right capabilities to meet business needs. Research suggests an arduous journey.
    - 30% of business leaders believe HR has a reputation for sound business decisions
    - 28% of business leaders feel HR is highly efficient
    - 22% believe that HR is adapting to the changing needs of the workforce
    - 20% believe that HR can adequately plan for the company's future
- The upshot: As business is growing and changing exponentially, HR is improving at a much slower pace.

The challenges are abundant, just as they are for CEOs and other business leaders in the spotlight. In 2013, almost 24% of Fortune 500 CEOs were replaced, so they evidently did not meet expectations or have the right capabilities either. One of the keys to getting better is to improve the talent and capabilities of the people in HR. This is difficult, especially because HR has such a poor record of improving itself. Bersin estimates that only 15% of organizations have HR developmental programs in place.

But the opportunity for HR to drive business results is not just about improving HR talent and capabilities, although this is a sizeable component.

There are three other next steps that must be taken. The first is *Building Professional Networks and Communities* to gain access to wisdom and tacit knowledge of seasoned professionals. Second, there must be practical ways forward. There are tangible *Levers* that HR can influence that directly impact alignment, cost savings and revenue improvements. Finally, it is essential to adopt the right *Mindset.* After decades of the perceptions that undercut the importance of HR, it is little wonder that HR has a confidence problem. If HR doesn't speak up and act courageously, all the talent and tacit knowledge in the world will be useless.

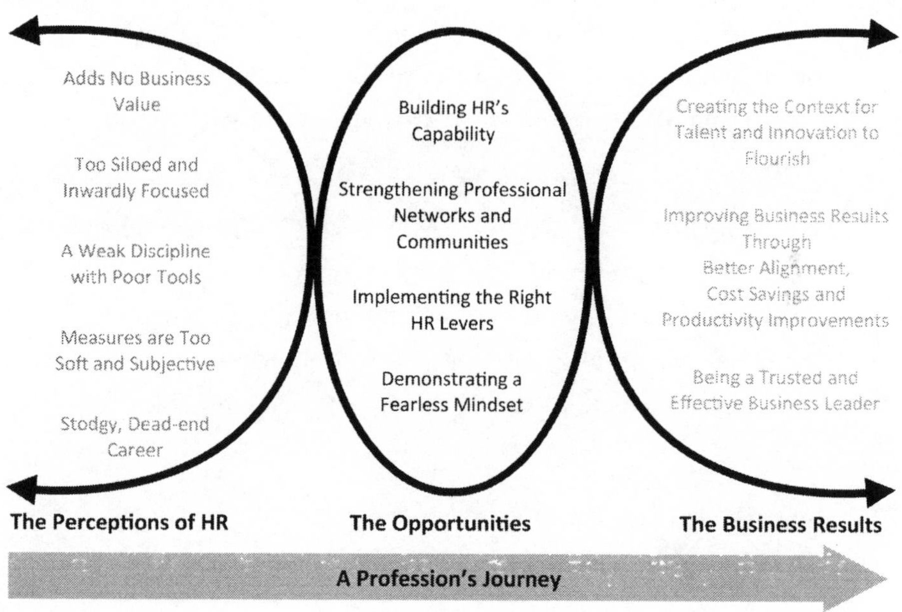

THE CURRENT-FUTURE STATE GAP FOR HR: RECOMMENDATIONS FOR YOUR PERSONAL JOURNEY

The future vision for HR, as espoused in *Fearless HR*, is to drive business results. The succeeding chapters in Part Two will describe this future vision in more detail and present four opportunities that can lead to achieving these goals. The magnitude of change from the current state to this future vision will vary for each organization and person. If the gap is significant, then the change process will be significant as well. If the difference between the current and future states is not great, then the journey will likely be smoother.

Thankfully, there is a body of knowledge that can provide guidance on change management and the likely resistance to be encountered. Through the work of John Kotter, the Heath Brothers, Robert Sutton and Huggy Rao, there are some principles to consider for your own professional journey.

- **Not Everyone is On Board.** Dave Ulrich has estimated that in any change initiative there is generally a 20-60-20 normal curve distribution, with equal percentages of people that embrace the change with those that fight it. The large group in the middle is on the fence and can go either way depending on the smoothness of the process. Not all HR professionals will embrace the change to becoming more strategic and a business leader. They don't see the compelling reason to change and do not want to deviate from their comfort zone. ***Decide where you stand.***

- **The Magnitude of Change Matters.** Anthropologists have long studied the process by which people adapt to new cultures and situations. The U-Curve plots cultural adjustment state of mind (emotions) over time moving from honeymoon to culture shock (crises) up through adjustment as depicted in Figure 6-1.

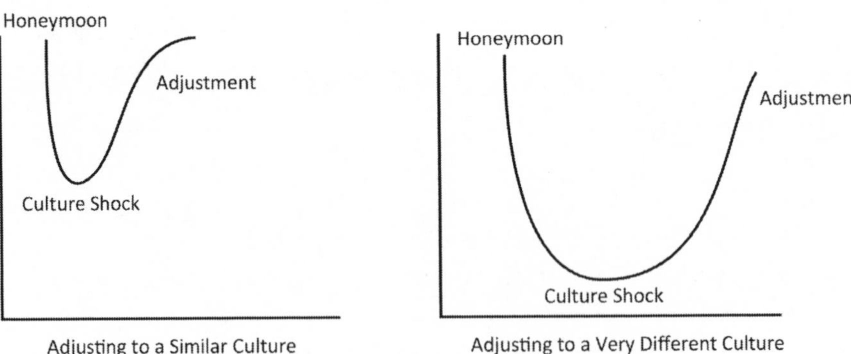

Figure 6-1: U-Curves for Adjusting to Similar and Very Different Cultures

The amplitude and wavelength of the U-Curve varies with the difference between the current and new situation. Thinking about cultures, if, for example, you are an English citizen going to Canada or Australia, the U-Curve will have different properties than if you are on assignment to Indonesia or Ecuador. The latter countries with different languages and cultural norms require a great deal more adjustment than the former countries. The same principle applies to the changes that HR must traverse to drive business results: if you are already practicing some of these changes, your adjustment period will require less time and difficulty. ***Understand the changes that you need to make.***

- **Break Change into Manageable Chunks.** A big transition can be intimidating. Understanding your strengths and where you are in the current-future state gap, enables you to focus on smaller changes that are accomplishable. The Heath brothers use the example of having to cut 5% from a budget. This can seem huge, but if the team focuses on two to three budget lines at a time, it becomes a more achievable task. Small successes for goals within immediate reach can be very meaningful and motivating. ***Shrink the change.***

- **Compelling Reasons to Change.** Kotter has stated that building a sense of urgency for change is critical and that it is the single reason why 50% of change initiatives fail. Without a firm belief that the status quo is absolutely unacceptable, people will be less willing to accept the disruption that accompanies divergent change. This condition is also referred to as *"the burning platform,"* and it needs to exist for the people impacted by change. The reasons for change are often clear to management, but not to the people expected to change. ***Be an advocate for and reinforce the need for HR's new role.***

- **Analyze-Think-Change vs See-Feel-Change:** After studying change projects for decades, John Kotter has come to the conclusion that data alone do not provide a compelling case to change. Because change involves emotions, *"See-Feel-Change"* has a much higher likelihood of success. The Heath brothers came to the same conclusion as they state that change involves both our rational and emotional selves, and we need to both Direct the Rider (rational) and

Motivate the Elephant (emotional). When changes fail, it is often because the Rider simply can't keep the Elephant and its emotional energy on the road long enough. Both selves need to be engaged, but we often try to over intellectualize change and underappreciate the emotional aspects. ***Deal with the emotional aspect of change.***

- **Hot Causes and Cool Solutions:** Sutton and Rau (2014) asked their Stanford students to address a tough change issue: in this case, why only 10% of students on campus wear helmets while riding their bicycles. They focused specifically on the men's soccer team, a group that probably felt such precautions were not really necessary for athletes. The students presented safety statistics to the soccer team, and as shocking as the statistics were, they had no impact at all. The rational self wasn't enough. The students then created a campaign that shared stories, symbols, language and reasons for the safety practices. It was dubbed the *Watermelon Offensive* and it literally included smashed watermelons around the soccer field, posters of injured students with watermelons in place of their heads, and small pictures encased in plastic and attached to the handlebars of each player's bike. This experiential communication strategy worked, and players actually signed a pledge to throw a watermelon at a teammate who flaunted the new rules. Other athletic teams at Stanford soon followed suit. ***Use the power of stories and experiences.***

- **Change is Scary:** There is no question that change takes you to an uncertain place. It is more comfortable being in a safe, known routine; but that sanctuary is increasingly unrealistic today. Change isn't an exception anymore, it is the new rule. And in dealing with change, it is helpful to recognize your own emotions as you go up and down the U-Curve of adaptation to new situations. It is also important to appreciate that the period of Culture Shock, although discomforting, is actually beneficial as it drives learning and eases assimilation. ***Know your own compelling case and keep it fresh.***

- **Paint a Picture of the Future.** Because change is altering the future, people have a right to know what the new vision is or might be. This vision may be adjusted as the new program or initiative is implemented, but it needs to be articulated. Kotter and the Heath brothers suggest vehicles such as an elevator speech, a destination postcard or a short newspaper article that describes the new vision and what it means to customers and employees. ***Craft a compelling future vision.***

Part Two of Fearless HR presents the opportunities that need to be taken for HR to drive business results. The order of these opportunities is important and sequential. It is now clear that there is nothing inherently wrong with the HR profession, and that old, historic perceptions are just that: old and not substantiated. HR, in fact, can be a major contributor to a great company if the following actions are taken:

- ☑ **Improve HR talent levels and capabilities**
- ☑ **Develop and expand professional networks**
- ☑ **Use HR levers to strengthen alignment, save costs and improve productivity**
- ☑ **Demonstrate a fearless mindset**

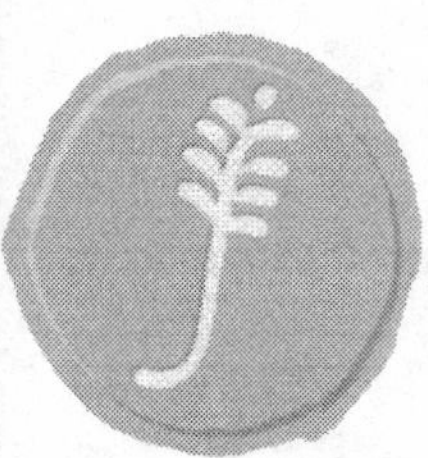

Chapter 6

Building HR's Capability

> *"In times of drastic change, it is the learners who inherit the future. The learned usually find themselves equipped to live in a world that no longer exists."*
>
> *Eric Hoffer*

Every department, function or profession shares the desire to improve capabilities and talent levels. Standing pat is simply not an option in this fast-paced, often turbulent period in which entire industries are turned upside down and companies must reinvent themselves regularly. Even relatively mature companies depend on products that didn't exist a year ago for the majority of its revenues. Change is a constant.

HR professionals understand that they are in a continuing battle to improve. They understand that their profession has been criticized for not being responsive or changing as fast as the business itself is changing. They know, in Marshall Goldsmith's terms, "*what got you here, won't get you there.*"

> *"HR has evolved, and so too have the people leading human development and performance. Long gone are the days when power hungry administrators place a death grip on all things necessary and rational. Today's CHROs don't gate progress; rather they are often the change agent fueling growth and development. In my work with CEOs it is not at all uncommon to find successful organizations where the CHRO is the closest and most trusted thought partner to the chief executive – this was not the case even a few years ago."*
>
> *Mike Myatt, Forbes, February 2015*

So, how do HR professionals strengthen and improve the capabilities needed to impact the business? What do HR professionals need to do to drive business results and play the roles that Myatt suggests? Let's first examine HR competency models to begin to answer these questions.

HR Competency Models

Competencies refer to the knowledge, skills and abilities (KSAs) demonstrated by individuals who do excellent (not average) work. Their use stems back as far as World War II, and got a jump start when David McClelland published his famous paper: *"Testing for competence rather than for intelligence."* Without competencies (and their associated key performance indicators), hiring, performance, and developmental discussions would remain too general to be meaningful and useful.

A number of HR competency models have been developed over the years. The most comprehensive and enduring is the HR Competency Study (HRCS) performed by the RBL (Results Based Leadership) group, beginning in 1987 and now in its seventh iteration.

The first HRCS competency model in 1987 had just three broad competencies: Business knowledge, HR delivery and Change. In 1997, the Culture competency was added, and the study also determined that Business Knowledge and HR Delivery had a lower impact on HR professionals overall competency. In the 2002, the new competency of Strategic Contribution was added as was a new HR Technology competency. This study reported that two competencies—Strategic Contribution and Personal Credibility—explained 60 to 70% of both individual and business performance.

The 2008 study again reinforced the significance of The Credible Activist as being the most impactful competency, but this study also showed that ***20% of a business's success can be attributed to HR professionals.*** This is a hugely important finding that has gone largely unnoticed, perhaps because it was part of an HR competency study that is mainly read by an internal HR audience.

In 2012, over 20,000 respondents participated in this global survey to define the characteristics of successful HR professionals. It is important to note that the sample also includes non-HR professionals so that external perspectives were also gathered and analyzed. The principal researchers and authors for these HRCS studies are Dave Ulrich, Wayne Brockbank, Dani Johnson, Kurt Sandholtz and Jon Younger.

2008 HR Competency Study	2012 HR Competency Study
Strategy Architect	Strategic Positioner
Talent Management and Organizational Designer	Capability Builder
Culture and Change Steward	Change Champion
Business Ally	Technology Proponent
Operational Executor	HR Innovator and Integrator
Credible Activist	Credible Activist

Figure 6-2: HR Competency Study Conducted in 2008 and 2012 (RBL Group, 2012)

The RBL authors have more recently highlighted six key domains that have emerged from their various studies over time as well as other competency models they have reviewed. Their article entitled *"Toward a Synthesis of HR Competency Models: The Common HR "Food Groups" or Domains."* will be published in HRPS People & Strategy. These six common domains are:

- Business
- Human Resource Tools, Practices and Processes
- HR Information Systems

- Change
- Organization and Culture
- Personal

As valuable as competency models are, they have limitations as well. They can be esoteric, expensive, overly complex and repetitive. Even if a company selects the option of using an existing competency library as opposed to conducting a dedicated research study, it can still be time consuming; and the final set of competencies may not be particularly distinctive. If everyone picks the same competencies from a library, how is my organization any different? Indeed, some researchers have found that 70% of leadership competencies are similar across organizations.

But the biggest issue with HR competency models is that they are internally focused. They make sense to HR professionals, but not to business leaders. Executives are more concerned with solving business problems, strengthening the organization and driving business results; and it is often unclear how just an HR competency model can contribute to these goals. This picture changes considerably, however, when *"capabilities, not just competencies"* are discussed. Ulrich and colleagues (2008) define the difference between the two terms: competencies relate to the individual and capabilities pertain to the collective abilities of an organization.

THE HR CAPABILITY FRAMEWORK (HRCF)

The HR Capabilities Framework (HRCF) combines both capabilities and competencies into a single framework that is relevant to business leaders and HR professionals alike. It also shows the relationship between the competencies that must be developed in order to drive the capabilities (business results and roles) that business leaders expect. Without improving the necessary competencies, HR could not effectively make a business impact.

The HRCF, then, is a hybrid framework that speaks to many audiences and yet provides clarity on "what needs to be accomplished" for HR to seize the opportunity before it. A competency model, by itself, would not be sufficient because it has little value to business leaders; and a capability model, by itself, would be too general to provide a path forward. The real strength of the HRCF is combining both perspectives so that HR can indeed fulfill the purpose of driving business results. Figure 6-3 defines the two main clusters of the HRCF: The HR Capability Cluster and The Foundational Competency Cluster.

HR CAPABILITY CLUSTER

Business Results	HR Roles
Create the Context in which Talent and Innovation Flourish	Strategic Architect
Improve Business Results through Better Alignment Cost Savings and Productivity Improvements	Force Multiplier
	Network Builder
Become a Trusted and Effective Business Leader	Operational Executor

Personal Qualities	Functional Excellence	Business Savvy
Passion for the Job	Talent Management	Business Acumen
Influence and Trust Builder	Compensation and Benefits	Financial Literacy
	HR Technology	
Continuous Learner	Legal Compliance	Data-driven Decisions
Humbition	Global Operations	Consulting Skills

FUNCTIONAL COMPETENCY CLUSTER

Figure 6-3: The HR Capability Framework

It is important to understand the derivation of the HR Capability Framework (HRCF) as presented in *Fearless HR*. It is *not* the result of a comprehensive research study, nor a synthesis of many different competency studies. Instead, the HRCF comes from my own reading of the industry and from countless conversations with practitioners and HR thought leaders over the years. These are my observations, supported by the wisdom of others, that I am asking you to consider; and because the HRCF is not research-based, you should feel free to add other capabilities and competencies that pertain to your organization.

But what is abundantly clear is that the HR profession must be able to articulate "what HR must do better" so that it can fulfill the purpose of driving business results. The HRCF--because it addresses capabilities and competencies together and speaks to both business and HR leaders--provides the standards for future HR development initiatives.

HR Capability Cluster: Business Results and HR Roles. This part of the Framework delineates what HR can become. It is the part of most interest to CEOs, Boards of Directors and fellow business leaders. There are two capabilities that comprise this cluster. The first is the business results that HR can deliver and the second is the roles that HR professionals play to make these results happen.

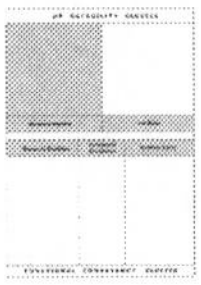

Business Results: There are three ways in which HR can drive business results. The first is to create the context in which talent and innovation can flourish. Business leaders look to HR to provide the guidance and tools to optimize the placement of talent. They want to know that the workforce has the right set of capabilities to be successful; and they want to know that the right person has the right skills and is in the right job (for the right cost at the right time in the right place). The second driver is delivering on business results. Usually HR is associated with reducing costs through such activities as reorganizations and staff reductions, but these are only a fraction of what can be contributed through clearer strategic alignment and improved productivity. And the third driver is truly being accepted as a trusted and effective business leader.

Business Results	Create the Context in which Talent and Innovation Can Flourish	Improve Business Results through Better Alignment, Cost Savings and Productivity Improvements	Become a Trusted and Effective Business Leader
Description	This is the classic talent management responsibility to improve the workplace and workforce. It is helping to ensure that the company has the right talent and culture to succeed. The 6Rs.	HR has many levers to improve business results. HR can reduce costs, but it can also add value by improving productivity and strengthening strategic alignment. All three are necessary.	This level of leadership transcends HR functional excellence. It is executive leadership for the whole enterprise. The HR leader has the same objectives and accountabilities as other members of the executive team.
Key Indicators	Analyzes the workplace Leverages success. Fixes problems. Promotes collaboration. Enhances engagement. Provides growth opportunities for employees. Matches top talent to the most critical roles Encourages internal moves. Builds flexibility into the workplace. Anticipates future needs and capabilities. Defines the desired culture. Moves the culture from the current to desired state.	Analyzes business performance. Aligns activities to strategy. Reduces costs. Improves productivity. Increases revenue. Strengthens profits. Improves earning per share. Improves the triple bottom line.	Sets direction. Removes barriers and roadblocks Inspires others. Seeks feedback. Marshalls resources. Delivers results. Is open and transparent. Moves proactively. Manages change. Executes successfully.

Figure 6-4: Impacts of HR

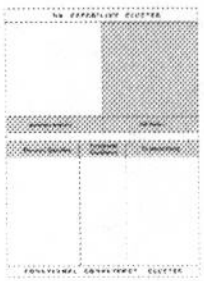

HR Roles: The HR Roles are means to achieve business results. The HR Roles are generally of interest to other business leaders because they are more likely to be expressed in the language of the business than generic competencies. The first HR role is *Strategic Architect.* This signifies that HR is firmly in the strategic camp and that, as an architect, HR analyzes function, relationships, patterns and structure of the organization. The second HR role is as a *Force Multiplier.* HR professionals have the opportunity to influence the organization beyond what their individual contribution would suggest. By shaping the environment to, for example, improve engagement and working to improve the skills of managers, HR's impact can be leveraged and magnified. The third role is for HR to be a *Network Builder.* This role increases collaboration, sense of community, and innovation across the organization. It emphasizes that an organization can be greater than the sum of its parts, if it breaks down barriers and works together. And the fourth role is *Operational Executor.* While HR can and must play in the strategic arena, it must also deliver on its operational tasks. As the Cisco case study in Chapter 5 demonstrated, the two are closely intertwined; and that strategic opportunities are only possible if transactional services are delivered effectively.

HR Roles	Strategic Architect	Force Multiplier	Network Builder	Operational Executor
Description	From RBL study. Being proactive, seeing a larger picture and how the pieces fit together. Being a lead time ahead.	The ability to optimize talent, find leverage points, improve the workplace and build on successes.	The connective tissue of the organization. Building networks and communities. Enhancing collaboration.	From RBL study. HR must deliver on transactional services, employee advocacy and make things happen.
Key Indicators	Thinks strategically. Aligns actions to strategy. Executes strategy. Anticipates potential problems. Anticipates industry shifts. Magnifies strengths. Minimizes weaknesses. Improves working relationships among groups. Improves competitive advantage.	Analyzes data Determines what works. Shines a spotlight on success. Takes action on engagement results. Removes barriers. Builds in more choices and options. Coaches managers. Manages change. Champions culture.	Works with different groups. Works on cross-functional teams. Acts as a network hub. Grows own network. Encourages others to grow networks. Recognizes hubs and connectors. Builds communities. Promotes grounds-up input. Participates in social media communities.	Implements HR services effectively. Gathers data on employee satisfaction. Responds quickly. Anticipates questions. Removes barriers. Treats employees as customers.

Figure 6-5: The Roles of HR

Foundational Competency Cluster: The Foundational cluster equips HR professionals to fulfill the key roles and achieve business results. This layer provides the needed infrastructure, and does resemble more traditional HR competencies. There are three layers in this cluster. The first layer is the Personal Qualities of HR professionals. These qualities should be considered when hiring and developing HR talent. The second layer is Functional Excellence which pertains most directly to the Operational Executor role previously described. These services must be provided seamlessly throughout the organization. The third layer is Business Savvy and these skills must be demonstrated before HR professionals can be credible and effective as both HR and business leaders.

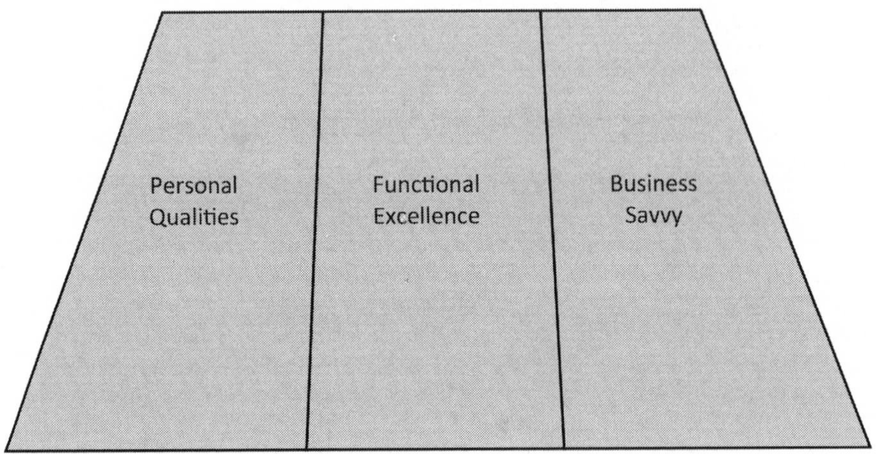

Figure 6-6: The Foundational Competency Cluster

Personal Qualities: There are four qualities that define an ideal team member, HR professional, and leader. It would be advantageous, for example, to follow a leader who is passionate about the job, builds trust, is always wanting to learn and grow, and who works with others to make the business successful. While these personal qualities can be developed and grown, it is also recommended that they be included as part of the hiring profile so that people are already demonstrating these qualities as they commence their new HR position.

Personal Qualities	Passion for the Job	Influencer and Trust Builder	Continuous Learner	Humbition
Description	Highly engaged and committed to the vision, mission and job. Positive energy.	This goes beyond communication skills. It means influencing internal and external audiences and developing a trust-based relationship with business leaders.	Never being satisfied and always looking to improve skills and gain new experiences.	From Collins Level 5 leadership. A person who is humble but gets results. Not about personal ego, but business success. Humble ambition.
Key Indicators	Sees job as a purpose. Enjoys coming to work. Has a positive impact on others. Strives to make a difference. Believes in providing services to others. Aligns to the company's mission and values. Gains satisfaction from doing a good job. Is involved in company activities.	Listens well. Asks meaningful questions. Pays attention to others. Is attuned to other's positions. Is buoyant. Has empathy for other's position. Makes compelling cases. Follows through on commitments. Has best interest of others in mind. Extends trust to others.	Is inquisitive. Asks good questions. Seeks new experiences. Enjoys learning. Wants to continually improve. Encourages others to learn. Looks for more challenges. Wants to build a stronger resume.	Is not ego driven. Commits to the company's progress. Drives for results. Perseveres in spite of obstacles. Keeps commitments and delivers on promises. Works well with others. Is trusting and transparent. Provides opportunity for others.

Figure 6-7: Personal Qualities

Functional Excellence: These are core HR skills. It is expected that these HR functions are efficient and effective, lead to high internal employee satisfaction, and are consistent with company goals and values. Strong internal expertise is needed to be effective in each of these areas.

Functional Excellence	Talent Management	Compensation and Benefits	HR Technology	Legal Compliance	Global Operations
Description	Able to hire, engage, develop and retain top talent, and employ effective talent practices.	Fair and equitable compensation and benefits with recognition programs for excellent performers.	Technology to make HR processes more efficient and effective.	Company policies and practices are lawful and fair. Proactively works to avoid legal claims and lawsuits.	Understands cultural perspectives while balancing standard and local needs.
Key Indicators	Reviews data on talent practices. Knows best practices. Conducts effective recruiting programs. Conducts effective engagement programs. Conducts effective learning and development programs. Conducts effective management and leadership programs.	Reviews data on talent practices Knows best practices Provides competitive salaries. Manages salary administration . Provides competitive benefits. Assists employees in being more self sufficient. Orchestrates an equitable recognition program.	Streamlines HR processes. Provides meaningful HR analytics. Integrates separate HR systems. Increases self-service options for employees and managers. Improves employee satisfaction ratings.	Reviews data on compliance issues and claims Knows best practices Prevents legal issues proactively Reviews policies to be compliant Resolves issues quickly Settles complaints out of court Provides legal and compliance training for employees.	Reviews data on the global workforce. Knows best practices. Understand local markets and competitive pressures. Balances local versus company policies. Balances the workforce. Moves toward more local nationals.

Figure 6-8: Functional Excellence

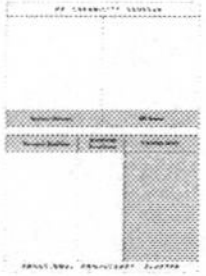

Business Savvy: If HR professionals do not speak the language of the business, they will not be successful, nor have credibility with other business leaders. HR professionals need to get out of their comfort zone to advance beyond internal processes and silos, add value from the outside, in; and drive business results. Specifically, the following skills and abilities must be sharpened:

- Business Acumen-- Understanding the bigger picture of the business and the value it provides in a fast-changing and competitive marketplace; and being able to help execute strategy.
- Financial Literacy—Recognizing and impacting the conditions that lead to financial health and positively influencing revenue, profit, costs and assets.
- Data-driven Decision Making—Using data to make better business decisions that leverage success and mitigate risk so that costs are reduced and productivity improves.
- Consulting Skills—Analyzing and solving business problems so that innovation and talent can flourish and business results are achieved.

Business Savvy	Business Acumen	Financial Literacy	Data-driven Decision Making	Consulting Skills
Description	The bigger picture of how the business works, and how money is made and value is delivered. Knows Industry trends and competitors.	The financial health of the organization based on company financial statements and the ability to make financial justifications for HR initiatives.	HR decisions need to be more evidenced-based and data-driven. HR decisions can be just as rigorous and disciplined as those in finance and operations.	Consultants focus on solving business problems. Consulting skills also emphasize the execution skills that are necessary to *"make things happen."*
Key Indicators	Knows company strategy. Articulates how the company provides value. Identifies key strategic initiatives. Aligns HR activities to strategy and outcomes. Describes key competitive differences Identifies strengths, weakness, opportunities and threats (SWOT).	Analyzes Income Statements. Analyzes Balance Sheets. Analyzes Cash Flow Statements. Suggests ways to improve revenue growth and profitability. Prepares a business case for the ROI of an HR initiative.	Analyzes data on the workplace and workforce. Segments these data to look for patterns and trends. Selects the meaningful data to build a scorecard and monitor across time. Acts on findings to improve the business by leveraging success or mitigating potential risks.	Asks good questions and listens well. Defines the right business problem, not just symptoms. Identifies all the stakeholders and audiences impacted. Gains agreement on expectations. Meets or exceeds expectations. Manages the change that will occur. Integrates lessons.

Figure 6-9: Business Savvy

DEVELOPING HR CAPABILITIES

Now that the HR Capability Framework (HRCF) has been established, it is possible to discuss how these HR skills can be improved. A simple answer would be to provide training on key skills, but this response would be inadequate based on the 70-20-10 model first proposed by Morgan McCall, Robert Eichinger and Michael Lombardo in the 1980s. As presented in Chapter 3, the authors believed that most learning occurs on the job, not in a classroom or in front of a computer terminal. They identified three types of learning: on the job experiences (70%), mentoring-coaching feedback (20%), and formal training (10%).

Today, however, the 70/20/10 formula has come under closer scrutiny. Most practitioners would still agree that experience is the best teacher, but alot has changed since the original formula was presented. Recent research by DDI and The Conference Board suggest a revised ratio of 55/25/20 (Talent Management, 2015). Forman and Keene (2013) propose doing away with the formula all together. Their other insights and recommendations follow:

- Learning doesn't occur from all experiences, especially if one is doing the same thing over and over again. *Learning occurs from new and different experiences* that challenge thought processes and lead to different approaches.
- A great deal of learning occurs *outside of work*. For example, increasingly companies are encouraging work on non-profit boards or in community activities as developmental assignments. Ulrich argues that 20% of learning comes from life, not just job experience.
- With the rise of Facebook and, especially, LinkedIn, personal networks have become vital sources of continued learning and development. These networks are based more on collegial rather than boss or formal coaching relationships.
- With the rise of Google, learning is much more than just factual recall—which is now at everyone's fingertips. Learning, instead, is more focused on application and higher-level thinking skills.

- Formal learning now includes a variety of advanced teaching methods and approaches, not simply didactic classroom or e-learning courses.
- Instead of a strict learning formula (such as 70-20-10 or 55-25-20) that has questionable validity, it is more useful to think of a portfolio of developmental opportunities. A Development Portfolio should include a range of different opportunities and experiences.

This concept of a *Development Portfolio* proposed by Forman and Keene will be applied to the two main HRCF clusters: The HR Capability and the Foundational Competency Clusters.

> *"I never try to teach my students anything.*
> *I only try to create an environment in which they can learn."*
>
> *Albert Einstein*

The first Development Portfolio deals with the HR Capability Cluster that includes Business Results and the Roles of HR.

Learning from New Experiences	Learning from Others	Learning from Courses, Materials and Interventions
Take a leadership position in a troubled group. Work on a difficult change management project. Open up a new global location. Guide an acquisition of a company through successful assimilation. Teach aspiring leaders. Participate in strategic sessions, earnings calls and executive meetings. Spend quality time with customers and partners. Take a developmental assignment in a non-profit organization. Lead a company, community-based, or volunteer initiative. Make presentations to internal and external audiences on strategic and leadership issues.	Be coached by a respected leader. Build a community of cross-functional leaders. Seek out colleagues who excel at cost savings. Seek out colleagues who excel at revenue growth. Seek out feedback, and advice from colleagues all levels. Visit companies that are leaders in their industries. Develop external networks. Participate in global groups and forums that address similar business issues. Participate in blogs and forums.	Analyze data and social media perspectives on the company (e.g. Glassdoor). Research analysts and industry reports on the company. Research key competitors. Review key websites on leadership and management innovations (e.g., HCI and management exchange.com). Read key news sources (everyday) for possible impacts on the company. Read key books and journals for ideas that can impact the company.

Figure 6-10: Development Portfolio for the HR Capability Cluster

The second Development Portfolio is for the Foundational Competencies that include personal qualities, functional excellence and business savvy.

Learning from New Experiences	Learning from Others	Learning from Courses, Materials and Interventions
Participate in cross-functional teams. Listen to earning calls and financial meetings. Meet with customers and value chain partners. Work on a major change initiative as a team member. Lead a cross-functional team. Participate in a research project and report results to management. Manage a project using outside consultants. Make a presentation to a group on the analysis of company human capital metrics. Participate in a technology implementation project. Take a global assignment. Work in global, cross-functional teams.	Be coached by a person with strong influencing and trust-building skills. Develop financial and operational buddies. Interview executives on the key business and financial issues the company faces. Interview experts in human capital analytics. Visit companies that are leaders in using HR analytics. Observe Level 5 leaders with "humbition" and record your observations. Work with consultants to better understand the HR technology marketplace. Interview the Chief Legal Counsel. Be coached by a respected global leader. Interview global employees after returning from a global assignment.	Review company financial and strategic statements. Research the company's competitive position. Research industry trends. Research analysts and industry reports on the company. Identify learning resources both internal and external. Attend industry conferences. Take courses to improve skill levels. Read key news sources (everyday) for possible impacts on the company. Read key books and journals for ideas that can impact the company.

Figure 6-11: Development Portfolio for the Foundational Layer Cluster

TAKING ACTION TO IMPROVE HR CAPABILITIES

The HR Capability Framework (HRCF) and the Development Portfolios are valuable resources for improving HR's skills and capabilities. The HRCF provides the end state and standards to which HR aspires. The Development Portfolios provide examples of the types of developmental activities that can lead to improving HR's talent and abilities. But these are just tools, and they need to be put to use as each person charts his or her own transitions.

We are all at different places in the journey to drive business results: 1) Create the context in which talent and innovation can flourish, 2) Improve business results through better alignment, cost savings and productivity improvement, and 3) become a trusted and effective business leader. It is necessary to craft your own path to become the most effective HR professional possible.

1. Start with a firm commitment to become a better and more effective HR professional. The journey starts with a mindset and emotional commitment. If you do not see the burning platform of why you must drive business results and get better, then you won't. Behaviors follow mindset. I was told decades ago by an early mentor that there are three reasons why people do not do what we want them to do: 1) they don't want to do it, 2) they can't do it, and 3) the system won't let them do it. The first reason tops everything else. The journey starts with your honest commitment.

2. Assess your strengths, weaknesses and progress in the journey. Each person brings unique assets and challenges to this journey, so everyone will have his or her own path. As we have seen, HR has many tools, models and frameworks it can use, and this is an ideal time to honestly assess your own skills and developmental areas. This assessment is not about intuition or preference; it is about gathering information, analyzing the data, reporting the findings and making recommendations....just as a consultant would.

3. Solicit a variety of data and feedback. By committing to a research and evidenced-based approach, the data gathered should go beyond simply your own views of strengths and developmental areas. This is an excellent opportunity to develop an instrument based on the HRCF and then provide it to colleagues.

Figure 6-12 is an example of a data gathering instrument that can be created based on the HR Capability Framework. In this case, the role of Force Multiplier was selected as a potential developmental area. Many of the key indicators for *Force Multiplier* (See Figure 6-6) are included in this survey; several were excluded because of length. This 360 degree instrument can be created quickly and easily because the indicators have already been delineated for each capability.

Then each audience (self, manager and peers) completes the rating (a five point scale with 5 being excellent and 1 being poor). When completed, this form shows the scores across audiences with the Peers rating being an average for all Peers surveyed.

HR Role: Force Multiplier	**Self***	**Manager***	**Peers***
Analyzes Human Capital Metrics for patterns of success and risk			
Takes action on engagement survey results			
Shines a spotlight on successes			
Takes action on potential risks before becoming a problem			
Builds in choices and options in the workplace			
Champions the desired cultural values			
Coaches managers to improve engagement			
Removes system barriers proactively			
Implements change initiatives effectively			

* A scale of 1 to 5, with 5 being excellent, 4 is good, 3 is average, 2 is fair and 1 is poor

Figure 6-12: An Example of a Survey Instrument Based on the HRCF

There will very likely be differences among groups which can then lead to insightful conversations. Research has often shown that the least reliable of these ratings is the self-rating, which is exactly why multiple perspectives and different sources of ratings are so important to gather.

4. Break down change into two or three manageable chunks. When the data have been gathered and analyzed, pick two or three areas to work on. The focus can be either to maximize strengths or improve weaker areas. Most people think it should be weaknesses only, but there is a body of research that says that more can be achieved by maximizing critical strengths. The literature on change advises that it is unwise to try to change too many things at once. Pick the *critical few* as opposed to the less consequential many.

5. Create six month development plans for improvements. Set targets and be accountable for results. The period of six months is about right as it creates a sense of urgency. If the time period is a year or longer, it can be easy to put off actions. Use the suggested activities in the Development Portfolios (Figures 6-11 and 6-12) presented earlier as guides in creating your own tailored development plan.

6. Assess actual (not just intended) progress through data and outcomes. After the six month period, it is time to evaluate progress. The easiest way to accomplish this is to re-issue the survey to the affected audiences and compare scores. This will provide comparable data to analyze. It is also possible to conduct focus groups and examine work products on the two to three focus areas. But most importantly, a variety data are gathered and analyzed to evaluate progress.

7. Either add more chunks or redouble efforts on previous goals. Recognize that this is a continual process. As we have said, a characteristic of a true professional is that improvement never stops. Being a *"continuous learner"* is built right into the HR Capability Model, and it is an essential quality because of the unrelenting change that organizations face. This *commitment to continuously improve* is a mindset and a belief that either exists or it doesn't. If it doesn't, then the original burning platform is not as compelling as first believed.

BRIDGING HR CAPABILITY GAPS

HR, like any profession or group, can achieve more with better talent. Just ask any director, conductor or athletic coach if they could use more talented players. They will probably add a few qualities beyond raw talent (such as Humbition); but their answer will be a resounding yes.

The HR Capability Framework provides a roadmap for improving the quality of HR talent. But one of the themes of *Fearless HR* is to take a step back, see the bigger picture, ask questions and apply some of the decision frameworks that HR has at its disposal. One question that could be asked is: Is this the only way to improve HR talent?

No, it is not. So far, the emphasis has been on building talent up internally; which is important but not the only avenue. In Chapter 3, the 7B decision framework was introduced. Ulrich and colleagues introduced the initial Bs to identify options for building capability within an organization. The most important options to improve HR capabilities are: Build-Buy-Borrow. The Build option is the one that has been pursued so far in this chapter. It has the advantage of providing career paths for others to follow who aspire to the same leadership levels. Its disadvantage is that it can take time to build capabilities, and in some cases, it may be time that doesn't exist.

The Buy option hires talent from outside the organization. This choice has the advantage, if hiring is done properly, of bridging the capability gap quickly. The rub is that many organizations do not have a great track record of effective hiring. Fully 40% of leadership hires fail within 18 months (an outrageous figure). Groysberg and colleagues studied the performance of star financial analysts and determined that when a star performer moves from one company to another, performance declines. Talent is therefore highly context sensitive.

The Borrow choice brings people and their capabilities from other departments, companies or consultants (note: some will view internal moves from other groups –outside of HR--as buying talent; but because this is often a temporary assignment, it will be considered borrowed talent). Again, the success of this option is based on making the right choices of talent and partners to use. If the borrowed talent is internal, there will likely be less adjustment because the culture and systems are known. But if the borrowed talent is truly transitory, the improved capability may not be sustainable.

There are strengths and limitations to each option. They must be used intelligently, and not because something must be done quickly. It is the 7th B—Balance—which really is the most crucial: What *should be* the right mix Build-Buy-Borrow to minimize risk and make the organization successful?

A Google Perspective

Laszlo Boch has thought long and hard about the right balance and mix of HR talent, including HR leaders. He echoes the views of Ram Charan, Dave Ulrich and the latest Deloitte Research: more companies are reaching into the ranks of different groups—operations, engineering, finance and even legal—to fill top HR position. Laszlo cites colleagues at Target, UPS, Microsoft, and eBay who have taken such a path. His reflection is that CEOs want a business orientation and analytical skill set that is not common with HR professionals.

Boch offers further advice to build an unconventional and diverse HR team. His current People Operations group includes global team members who collectively speak more than 35 languages and come from very different backgrounds. He says quite candidly: *"in the HR profession it is an error to hire only HR people."* His solution, again keeping in mind the culture and business of Google, is the *"three thirds"* hiring model.

1. The first third is HR professionals hired for their functional excellence, influencing skills, practical orientation and ability to recognize patterns in people and organizations.

2. The second third is from top-tier strategy (not HR) consulting firms. Strategy consultants are preferred because they have a deep understanding of the business and excel at solving tough problems. It is, however, essential that these consultants have strong EQ and team communication skills. These may not always be present in every top-tier consultant.

3. The final third is people who are deeply analytic, holding at least a master's degree in an analytical field. These individuals ensure that the analytics and research are robust, systematic and valid.

4. Then, mix the groups. Everyone gets different opportunities to contribute and learn from each other.

Lessons Learned: Shared Purpose, the Right Profile, Diverse Teams, Cross-functional Rotations

While not every organization has the resources to follow Google, there are certainly several principles that should be replicated. First, the overall aspiration and role of HR should be understood and shared by all. In *Fearless HR*, this vision is that *HR drives business results*. This shared understanding establishes positive mindsets and expectations. Second, HR must have a very clear understanding of the most significant skills and abilities needed in the HR organization. Boch's *three thirds* hiring model is intentional and very consistent with the charter and shared purpose of People Operations at Google.

Third, create a diverse HR team and there are several reasons for doing so. First, the HR team should be a reflection of the people in the orbit of the organization, including employees, customers, partners and shareholders. As an organization increases its global presence, there is the need for a similar representation in HR. And second, the research is very clear that heterogeneous groups lead to different ideas and more innovation than homogeneous teams. Diverse groups can be more challenging to manage, but the payoffs are significant. The more the workplace looks like the marketplace, the higher the likelihood that new connections and value will be created.

A final staffing and deployment guideline is to, in Boch's words, *mix it up*. The wisdom of this approach is clear. Engagement improves as people are given new challenges outside of their comfort zone. As engagement goes up, so does productivity. The organization becomes more agile and effective as multiple people have back-up skill sets; and individuals become more marketable—either internally or externally—because they have added valuable skills and experiences. Cross-functional teams and rotations build networks and expand influence.

Summary

It is essential to continue to build HR's capability and talent levels, as it would be for any profession aspiring to be a respected business leader. Given HR's past, the journey may be a bit longer and more arduous than most, but it is essential. *Building HR's Capability* is the first opportunity discussed in Part Two because without accomplishing this goal, the other opportunities won't matter. HR professionals must be able to deliver the *"goods."*

The HR Capability Framework (HRCF) presents a tangible representation of what HR can become. Its three business drivers send a clear message to other executives of HR's contributions. HR's job is to: create the context in which talent and innovation can flourish, improve business results, and become a trusted and effective leader. The HRCF provides a pathway to achieve these impacts through supporting capabilities and competencies. It is then possible to create Development Portfolios that can be used by HR professionals to grow and further develop these important foundations.

In *"Taking Action to Improve HR Capabilities,"* a step-by-step approach is presented for HR professionals to use these tools to make their own transitions. Using tools such as the HRCF, Development Portfolios, and lessons from change management projects, a data-driven approach to personal improvement is both possible and preferred.

Taking a step back to consider the broader question of bridging capability gaps, other HR models can be employed. The Build-Buy-Borrow model suggests other possibilities could be utilized depending on timeframes and criticality of the need. The Google experience also suggests different staffing models and approaches to ensure that HR has the right talent levels going forward.

But we are not done yet. It is essential to Build Capabilities, but there are other opportunities that can further enhance HR's credibility and ability to drive business results.

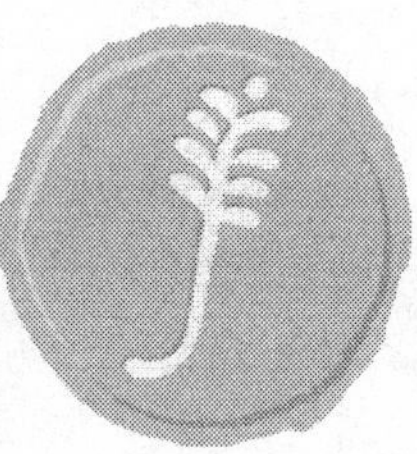

Chapter 7

Strengthening Professional Networks and Communities

> *"Ain't none of us as smart as all of us."*
>
> *Satchel Paige*

As organizations move into uncertain futures, they need leaders and professionals who are agile, continuous learners and creative problem solvers. As entire industries are shifting right in front of our eyes—newspapers, broadcast television, healthcare, banking, among others—it is the ability of people in these organizations to understand the change, adjust and adapt that determines future success and failure.

In Chapter 6, the HR Capability Framework was presented as a means to improving the capability and talent in the HR profession. Much of this learning comes from new experiences, using Google and other web tools, and attending courses and conferences. But increasingly, valuable insights are derived from people that we know—colleagues in professional networks and communities we frequent. As social beings, we like to seek out connections and learn from other people. This lesson is abundantly clear in the social media tools used in our personal lives. Facebook now counts 1.4 billion users around the world (April, 2015), with 936 million daily active users including 31% of all seniors within the United States. LinkedIn targets the business and professional audience, and it now totals over 350 million users in 200 countries, 70% of these users are outside of the United States.

There is also an organizational need for greater connections and collaboration. As organizations become larger, bureaucracies and siloes emerge which restrict synergies and collective energies. It becomes increasingly difficult to reach across boundaries, enlist the aid of others, leverage resources and get things done. Gary Hamel (2008) recognizes this reality very clearly: *"Communities outperform bureaucracies every day of the week."*

This lack of leverage drives CEOs crazy. Most large companies have a goal to be "one company" in which knowledge, talent and resources are shared. But the opposite often happens, especially when leaders lack *"Humbition"* and are more concerned with power, prestige and position. Lew Platt, an ex-CEO of Hewlett Packard, expressed his frustration about this lack of collaboration in now iconic words. *"If HR only knew what HP knows, we would be three times more profitable."*

The Importance of Building Professional Networks and Communities

Seth Godin is a thought-leader who challenges past ways of thinking that may not apply to the new digital, web-centric world. He talks of the emergence of *"the connection economy"* and how value is created by the connections we make, not by resources, tangible assets or having more stuff. He urges companies to think about making more connections with employees, partners, and customers; and then how to make these connections, not just casual but meaningful. Godin even goes so far as to suggest that leaders should be Chief Connection Officers.

The theme of forming strong connections is evidenced in this story about the value of a Harvard education (the story works with any prestigious university or college, so feel free to make a substitution if desired). The story goes that the value of a Harvard education is not *what you've learned, but who you've met.* It is most certainly an exaggeration, but there are elements that ring true.

A similar distinction is made in trying to categorize the value that people bring to an organization. Weatherly has termed this *asset "intangible capital."*

Type of Intangible Capital	Description	Examples
Human Capital	The collective knowledge, experience and attributes of employees.	Competencies Know how
Structural Capital	The codified knowledge that resides within an organization.	Intellectual property Patents Methodologies
Social Capital	The relationships within the organization to facilitate the transfer of knowledge.	Team relationships Collegial networks Know-who
Organizational Capital	The company's external relationships.	Customers Brand credibility Distribution channels

Figure 7-1: Types of Intangible Capital

While human capital is the term most often heard, social or relational capital is gaining in prominence. It is not just *know how*, but *know who* that defines the contributions that can be made.

The difference between *explicit and tacit knowledge* was first described by philosopher Michael Polanyi in 1958. In his subsequent work he said that *"We can know more than we can tell"* which begins to describe the difference between explicit and tacit knowledge (as well as sounding very similar to Lew Platt's comments on Hewlett-Packard). Explicit knowledge is knowledge that can be written down and easily transferred. It is most often information, data, documents, records and files. It is also referred to as *"know-that"* because it is fact-based knowledge that often exists in books or documents that can be accessed by other people. By contrast, tacit knowledge resides within each person or team, is not easily codified; and includes such knowledge types as experience, intuition, lessons learned, rules of thumb, insights, wisdom and *know-how.* The visual most often associated with tacit and explicit knowledge is the iceberg metaphor.

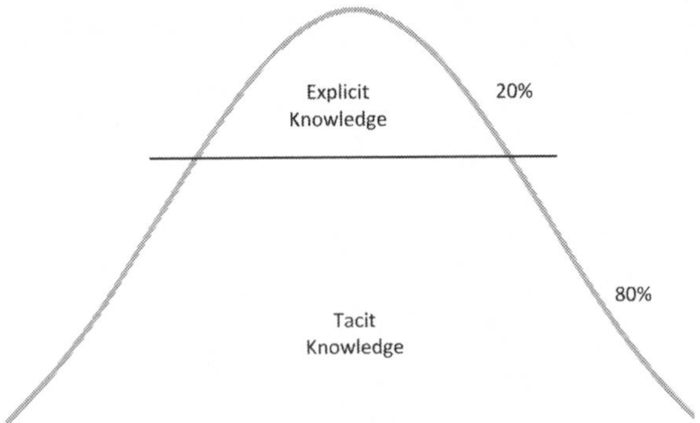

Figure 7-2: Tacit and Explicit Knowledge

The iceberg metaphor is appropriate because so much knowledge exits below the surface, locked up in our minds. While there are a variety of estimates for the balance between explicit and tacit knowledge, most place the balance at 20% explicit and 80% tacit.

Why is this seemingly academic discussion (started by a philosopher) meaningful to improving the capabilities of HR? The reason is that the key to unlocking the vast repository of tacit knowledge within people is building stronger professional networks and communities. Without these strong connections, great amounts of wisdom and insight are lost to organizations. Tacit knowledge gets awakened and shared through the give and take of conversations between HR professionals.

Industries with older workforces are now facing a major problem. As experienced senior people retire, their tacit knowledge goes with them. Some companies have tried to implement knowledge management systems to capture the knowledge of older workers. But these systems have only been marginally successful because they usually capture only explicit knowledge. It takes the human touch to cultivate the expression of tacit knowledge in others.

It is time for businesses to recognize that building professional networks and communities is a mission-critical HR role. It is not a nice to have, it is essential. Social capital is a major contributor to intellectual capital. The market popularity of Facebook and LinkedIn tell the story very clearly. It is also very apparent when you ask people how they use two resources available to them: Google and their personal network. The most often repeated answer is that Google is used when you want to know or check a fact (i.e., explicit knowledge), but if you really want to know what happened or how something works (tacit knowledge), you use your network.

Research on Professional Networks and Communities

Because of the success of social media networks and the awareness of the value of professional networks, there is a growing body of research and practice that can be referenced. Similar to the research presented in Part I of *Fearless HR*, these results are from different organizations and contexts so the findings may not directly apply to all situations; but it is nevertheless useful to be aware of this body of evidence and the trends, terms and insights that are starting to emerge.

1. **IBM research on the value of professional networks.** IBM found that professionals with larger professional networks were more productive (typically by about 10%) than colleagues whose networks were not as extensive.

2. **World War II Studies:** A series of studies were performed during World War II that focused on the primary motivations of combat soldiers. The researchers' hypotheses included such potential factors as patriotism, protecting loved ones back home and basic survival instincts. The biggest motivator, however, was not letting down the people in your platoon. These are the people—the community of brothers and sisters today—who shared the danger, experienced it every day, and depended on each other. Meeting the expectations of your fellow soldiers (in the small unit of the platoon) and with whom so much has been shared, was the strongest motivator for putting oneself in harm's way.

3. **Engagement Research:** We have already seen findings from the more than two decades of studies on engagement (see Chapter 1). The Gallup Q12 survey is a cornerstone of engagement research and has led to many important insights, including: *people join companies but leave managers.* But another interesting insight is the extent to which colleagues and co-workers matter. The following Q12 questions at least touch on this domain.

- In the last seven days, have I received recognition or praise for doing good work?
- Does my supervisor, or someone at work, seem to care about me as a person?
- Is there someone at work who encourages my development?
- Are my co-workers committed to doing quality work?
- Do I have a best friend at work?
- In the last six months, has someone at work talked to me about my progress?

Fully half of the Q12 address, directly or indirectly, the environment created by colleagues and teammates. The wording "*or someone at work*" is clearly intentional, and it implies that the feedback, recognition or conversation with colleagues is at least as important as those coming from the boss.

4. The Network Secrets of Great Change Agents (HBR, 2013). Battilana and Casciaro tracked over 60 change projects in Britain's National Health Service, and they isolated predictors of successful projects. They found that the personal network of change agents were instrumental to success. Furthermore, the credibility of change agents themselves and the meaningful role they played in the informal structure of the organization (not the formal org chart) was a clear advantage. And finally, the type of professional network and its fit to the situation made a difference.

The authors distinguish between *cohesive and bridging networks.* A cohesive network is comprised of people already connected to each other. They are likely in the same department or group, use similar language and have common understandings. Social cohesion leads to high levels of trust and support, and it is usually easier to manage a cohesive group. In a bridging network, as the name implies, you are connecting to people who are not connected to each other. This network is the bridge to different departments, groups, communities and people. New ideas and novel information are likely to emerge from bridging networks.

Battilana and Casciaro recommend that cohesive networks are best for implementing minor changes quickly, while bridging networks were best for instituting more drastic reforms.

5. Strength of Ties. Reid Hoffman is the CEO of LinkedIn and has obviously thought about networks and the difference between quick and meaningful connections. In his April, 2012 blog he writes about *"Allies and Acquaintances: Two Key Types of Professional Relationships."* Allies are people with whom a strong and trusting bond has been developed over time. An ally is someone you consult with regularly and proactively share information. Allies develop each other's personal brands and look for opportunities, together or separately. This is a true reciprocal alliance in which value is shared and exchanged. Hoffman suggests that it takes several years for an ally to form from an acquaintance.

There are many more acquaintances that impact a professional's life. Social scientists call acquaintances *"weak ties"* because contact is only occasional and exchanges are low-intensity. But weak ties are extremely valuable in expanding the breadth and reach of a network. A well-known study conducted in the 1970s found that more jobs were the result of referrals by acquaintances than colleagues with stronger ties. The research paper was titled *"The Strength of Weak Ties."*

Weak ties, just like bridging networks, provide access to different groups and perspectives. They also are a feeder system for potential Allies and the insight and tacit knowledge they possess.

6. The Contagion Effect. Tom Rath has written extensively on human behavior in business, health and well-being. In *"Are You Fully Charged"* (2015) he describes the Contagion Effect in relationships. Basically, this effect says that the people you spend time with influence your own behavior, habits and choices. The Contagion Effect is certainly present and influences *"self-fulfilling prophecies"* as discussed in Chapter Nine.

Much of the Contagion Effect research is about negative influences. For example, Cacioppo has found that the feeling of loneliness is transmitted via social networks. If a direct connection to you is feeling lonely you are 52% more likely to feel lonely as well. There are powerful influences that get transferred to others, whether intended or not.

Fortunately the Contagion Effect works in the positive direction as well. Rath offers the following advice.

> *"When you do something kind for another person, he or she is more likely to pay it forward, as is the next person. Almost any investment in another person has an exponential return beyond what you can see in the moment. Continue to create positive experiences for people."*
>
> *Tom Rath, 2015*

7. Organizational Network Analysis (ONA). Rob Cross at the University of Virginia has been studying the power of informal networks for two decades. ONA provides an x-ray into the inner workings of an organization. It shows patterns of communication, collaboration and information flow among people and strategically important groups. His research shows that appropriate connectivity in organizations leads to improved learning, performance and innovation.

ONA draws a sharp contrast between the formal and informal structures of an organization. The following example is taken from Rob Cross's web site.

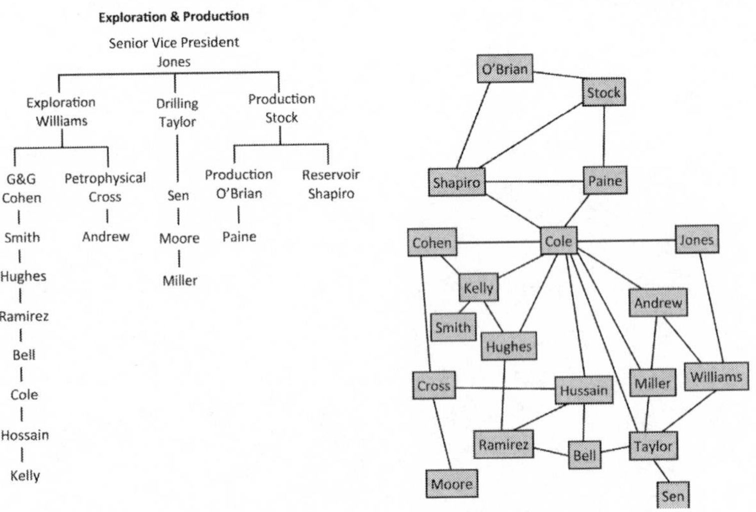

Figure 7-3: Formal and Informal Networks

There are several observations to make about this actual ONA performed on an oil and gas exploration company.

1. There is a very big difference between the formal organization chart and the way the company actually works. A great deal goes on in the white spaces of an organization.
2. It is clear that Cole is a central figure both in information flow and also as the only connector to the production team.
3. There are high level people in this company on the periphery of information sharing and collaboration. The highest ranking executive is Jones and he or she is not in the mainstream; perhaps this is by design, but possibly Jones and other leaders are too isolated.
4. The Production Group is largely off on its own, separated from the rest of the organization.

The people at the center of information flow and exchanges are often called hubs or connectors. There are, of course, several ways to interpret the hubs as their impacts may be positive or negative. The people on the periphery are often called nodes; and again, there are several possible interpretations of a node: perhaps the person lacks technical or social contact skills, or perhaps is an underutilized resource. But these answers can be determined with follow up analysis, and the insights gained from an ONA can be a positive influence on driving business results.

8. Criterion for High Potential Leaders and Job Candidates. Some companies are now using professional network size and strength as a criterion for selection as a high potential leader. This use is a clear recognition that network strength is of great value to the organization. During succession planning sessions, candidates are usually evaluated on both performance and potential. Performance is the easier of the two criteria to define and monitor. Potential refers to leadership potential, and usual criteria include:

- Ability to perform at higher levels in the organization within 18 months
- Learning agility
- Emotional intelligence
- Possible others: mobility, value alignment, handling complexity, teaching others
- New criterion: Strength of professional network

It is also interesting to note that increasingly recruiters are using a candidate's network strength as an explicit priority when hiring (Hoffman, Casnocha and Yeh 2014). The authors make the distinction between simply looking at the number of connections (network size) to being connected to the right people (network strength).

9. The Alliance and I^{we}. As noted previously, Reid Hoffman is the CEO and Founder of LinkedIn. He has a vested interest in promoting professional networks. But Hoffman is also one of the most influential thought leaders today, and his HBR article and book authored with Ben Casnocha and Chris Yeh are resonating with many people. Its title is *"The Alliance"* and its premise is that a new relationship is emerging between companies and employees. It is a reciprocal, mutually beneficial relationship, with explicit terms, in which both entities gain value. They advise that:

- *Employers need to tell employees: Help make our company more valuable and we will make you more valuable.*
- *Employees need to tell their bosses: Help me grow and flourish and I will help the company grow and flourish.*

While others have proposed a similar vision, the authors go on to propose some unique aspects to this mutually beneficial alliance. One suggestion is to hire people for explicit *tours of duty* and not to pretend that employees will stay with a company for decades. Research shows clearly that people move to different jobs often, so why do companies act as if this is a career-long decision? It isn't. Instead, it is possible to have an honest discussion about a four to five year *tour of duty* in which the employee can expect X, Y and Z; and the company can expect A, B and C.

But the primary contribution of *The Alliance* as it pertains to *Fearless HR* is to again herald the importance of professional networks. The simple little formula I^{we} says it all. In an earlier book by Hoffman and Casnocha, *The Start Up of You,* I^{we} meant that an individual's career accelerates with the strength of his or her network. So there is clear benefit to the individual employee. In a reciprocal relationship, there needs to be value to the company so the question becomes: Are employees willing to use their networks on behalf of the company? Their answer is yes. Fully three-fourths of high performers said they used their personal networks to help them on the job.

> *"To gain an edge, you need to use social networks to tap directly into what's swirling around inside people's brains. And it is this kind of information—up to the second and nuanced—that offers the most significant competitive advantage. You won't find it in the Wall Street Journal or even in a Google search. In a highly networked era, who you know is often more valuable than what you've read."*
>
> *Hoffman, Casnocha and Yeh, 2014*

One actual example that Hoffman, Casnocha and Yeh use to cement the power of networks is the common link among these successful companies: LinkedIn, Tesla, YouTube, Yelp, Yammer and SpaceX. They were all founded by alumni of a single company: PayPal.

10. Building Trust-based Relationships. Connections, just by themselves, are not inherently valuable. It is what you do with the connections that matters. It is the same for computer networks. Connections are the hardware part of an IT network, but it is the software (allowing for the exchange of information and active participation) that matters most. It is the same in a professional network. If the software is defective, you can't progress from an acquaintance to an ally or from a casual connection to a meaningful relationship.

Regardless if the professional network is virtual or in person, there is one condition that must be in place for meaningful exchanges to exist. That condition is trust. Trust is the secret sauce that makes professional networks work or stop. And while trust can be subjective, Covey (2006) has shown that it can be defined and that it has real business value. Among the indicators of a trusting relationship:

- Communicates honestly
- Keeps the best interest of others in mind
- Respects the contributions of each person
- Follows through on commitments
- Admits mistakes

Covey has also shown that high trust leads to quicker action and lower costs. He cites studies that show that high trust organizations outperform low trust cohorts by three to five times. He identifies seven business benefits of trust relationships: Increased value, accelerated growth, enhanced innovation, improved collaboration, stronger partnering, better execution and heightened loyalty. Trusting relationships drive business value.

11. Types of People in Your Network. There are a variety of ways to characterize the people in a professional network. As we have seen, there are acquaintances and allies, and there are cohesive and bridging members. There are also hubs and nodes in the information sharing diagrams of informal organizations.

It is important, however, to intentionally build a network to the ideal configuration. One clear criterion is *technical skills.* It is very valuable, for example, to have people who can provide knowledge and wisdom in important but unfamiliar competencies. Another criterion is to have a *diverse, as opposed to homogeneous, network* to help ensure complimentary skills and a wide variety of perspectives. Diverse networks provide a greater range of thought and are more likely to be innovative in their approach. Possible criteria for selecting diverse participants would be: different team roles (e.g., Belbin team roles), personality types (e.g., DISC), or cognitive styles (e.g., Meyers Briggs), in addition to demographic factors.

Mike Fishbein, author and blogger, has identified the *"Five Best Types of People to Have in Your Network."* His suggestions:

- Connectors: Leveraging connectors extends your reach tremendously.
- Experts: Adding to your capability and credibility.
- Rising Stars: Passing along your tacit knowledge to help others…..and they won't forget you later.
- Peers: Getting the best practical advice and feedback.
- Outliers: Including people totally outside your industry for fresh ideas and insights.

These are 11 different sources on research, information and advice on the value of professional networks. These sources may take different approaches, but the core message is the same. A professional network is a very valuable asset, both for the individual and the company. It can be truly reciprocal in the value it provides both parties.

TAKING ACTION TO IMPROVE PROFESSIONAL NETWORKS AND COMMUNITIES

The two most familiar models for the power of networking are very different. The first is the *CEO country-club model* that probably started at prestigious schools, continued through social clubs and long lunches, and was technology-averse. These networks were all about personal connections for the few, and while knowledge sharing and communication occurred, these networks existed for power and favor. The second model is *"Facebook, LinkedIn and other social media sites."* These sites are for the many (as in very many), have been facilitated by technology, and are largely for the purpose of keeping in touch, communicating and spreading the word. The average Facebook user has 250 friends in their web of connections.

A professional network is also about communications and knowledge sharing, but it is primarily about building capabilities and wisdom (tacit knowledge). The following are the action steps that can be taken to grow and develop a professional network.

1. Start with a firm personal commitment to develop and expand your professional network. This personal commitment is a prerequisite to doing the work necessary to strengthen your professional network. It takes time and effort to grow networks, and this process can occasionally take you out of the comfort zone, so you must firmly believe in the value of extending your professional network.

2. Assess the composition of your current network. Everyone has some kind of network, intended or not. Before improvements can be made, the current state needs to be identified. Gather data on the effectiveness, reach, and currency of the existing network. Analyze how information from the network is being used to improve capabilities and make better decisions. From this current state review, insights can be gained on needed improvements.

3. Review key development priorities from the six month development plan and incorporate your network. In the previous chapter, a commitment was made to a six month development plan focusing on two or three capabilities to grow further. Now, think specifically how your professional network can help to develop those capabilities. Who can provide wisdom, guidelines, tacit knowledge and access to others on these topics? Who could be a good coach or mentor? Adjust your development plan to include more entries in the *Learning from Others* column.

4. Intentionally expand your network: Commit to expanding your professional network by six to eight new connections each quarter. A network is a living thing; it needs care, cultivation and feeding. A network can be grown by adding to its reach or further developing the strength of connections. Here are some suggestions for ways in which networks can be expanded.

- Identify two to four new internal connections. These connections could be in cohesive or bridging networks.
- Identify two areas of expertise to develop further.
- Identify two external groups that you want to connect with. This bridging network extends your reach and visibility.
- Identify an influential thought leader or respected leader to meet. This step builds the quality and credibility of your network, even if the connection is just as an acquaintance.
- Identify one acquaintance to become a new ally. This step enriches an existing contact or acquaintance.

5. Continue to gather data to analyze the effectiveness and reach of your network. Learn from Facebook and LinkedIn. Gather data on your network, analyze it, look for patterns and make improvements. Your network is an ideal laboratory for experiments, pilot projects and evidence-based decision making.

TOOLS AND TEMPLATES

The following tools and templates can be used to identify, analyze and improve professional networks. Each tool can and probably should be customized and adjusted to particular contexts and circumstances.

Tool 1: Internal Cohesive Network: An Example

As we have seen, one way to characterize professional networks is the distinction between cohesive and bridging networks. A cohesive group shares common understandings, language, experiences and perspectives. There are typically high levels of trust and support within cohesive networks. In this tool, diagram all the members of a cohesive group and indicate the strength of relationship in three ways: 1) a double line indicates a strong relationship in which value is exchanged on a regular basis (an ally); 2) a single line indicates a person that you know and value, but don't interact with and share information on a regular basis (an acquaintance) ; and 3) a dotted line is someone that you do not yet know.

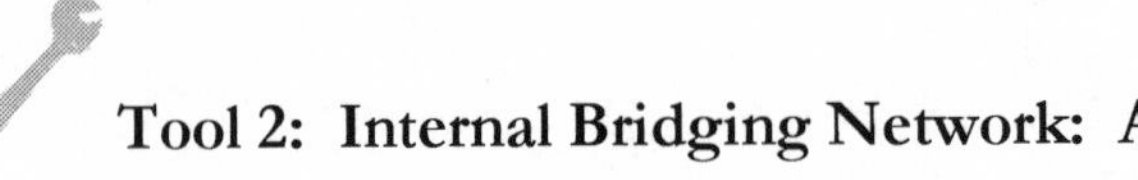

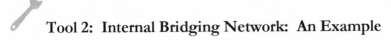

Tool 2: Internal Bridging Network: An Example

Bridging networks are connections among people that you typically do not know, and are therefore more heterogeneous than cohesive networks. There usually isn't common ground and shared understandings, and most of these connections will be acquaintances rather than allies. Bridging networks can greatly expand visibility and coverage. Diagram one or more bridging networks that you are connected to. The same network diagram conventions (double line, single line and dotted line for strength or relationship) are used in this example.

Tool 3: External Networks

As important as internal networks are, there are a lot more people outside an organization than inside. It is important to identify the various sources of external contacts and analyze which ones have been the most fruitful in expanding the breadth and depth of your network. Diagram two or three important external networks.

Tool 4: High Priority Contacts

It is easy to get distracted and be overwhelmed by the number of acquaintances and connections. But the strength of a person's professional network is not about quantity, but quality. A few great allies are worth their weight in gold, and these relationships must be cherished and expanded. This tool helps in prioritizing and growing the reciprocal relationship with the people that matter most.

High Priority Contact	Value Provided	Dates of Contact	Key Messaging

Tool 5: The Care and Feeding of Networks

Networks are relationships, and there are both practical and research-based findings on what makes a successful relationship. While these guidelines may seem to be common sense, they may not be common practice. Add your own guidelines and dos and don'ts to this list.

Positive Network Behaviors	Negative Network Behaviors
Be respectful	Say whatever is on your mind
Have others best interests in mind	Put your best interests forward
Listen	Present
Be authentic	Say what you think people want to hear
Let the conversations happen	Rush to judgment
View issues from the perspective of others	Push your experiences and knowledge
Be responsive	Wait until the time is right for you
Communicate frequently	Communicate sporadically
Seek solutions not just problems	Focus on the negative
Be visible and have regular updates	Go quiet once you get what you want
Do something for others	Do something for your self
Provide joint value	Take for yourself

Tool 6: Network Analysis

It is important to understand what your professional network is and is not. Just like Facebook and LinkedIn, there is a great deal to learn from examining analytics on a professional network. There are a variety of analytics that could be examined, but probably the most useful is to analyze the various sources of contacts and the contributions they make. While these data may not be exact, they can provide insight on the sources that lead to the greatest number of connections, allies, areas of specific expertise, connecting to connectors and access to new groups and communities.

Source	Allies and Acquaintances	Expertise	Connectors	New Groups
Internal Cohesive Groups				
Internal Bridging Groups				
LinkedIn				
Conferences and Classes				
SHRM, HCI and HR Communities				
Alumni				
Other Social Media				
External Friends				
Interest Groups				
Civic and Community Life				

Summary

Professional networks are incredibly valuable assets. For the individual, they contribute to a person's brand, visibility, reach, credibility, capabilities, tacit knowledge, influence and productivity. For an organization, professional connections can lead to greater capabilities, impacts and outcomes. When individual networks are utilized to improve organizational performance, a force-multiplier effect can be expected. This is a true reciprocal alliance in which both employees and organizations prosper.

It is time for the HR profession to recognize the incredible value associated with network and community building. Unlocking tacit knowledge can, by itself, make businesses more efficient, effective and impactful. We know that greater collaboration leads to innovation, so why not leverage this relationship? Social capital, as evidenced by networks and communities, is perhaps the greatest asset organizations have.

Chapter 8

Implementing the Right HR Levers

> *"Businesses don't create value; people do."*
>
> *Charan, Barton and Carey, 2015*

For HR to be successful in the dynamic, fast-changing world in which we live, HR professionals must continue to improve, set the bar higher and never be complacent. Improvement is primarily accomplished through ongoing development of those essential capabilities that enable HR to drive business results. Improvement also comes from expanding professional networks and communities as these unlock the tacit knowledge that resides in the minds of thought and opinion leaders.

But even if HR professionals are capable and *"ready"* to contribute at a higher level, it doesn't follow that they will do so. There is often a sizable difference between *knowing and doing* as Pfeffer and Sutton observed at the turn of the century. Stephen Covey has similarly suggested that organizations need to have higher xQs (execution quotients), not IQs: Heath and Heath (2010) observe that what often looks like a people issue in executing change projects is, in many cases, a situation problem. If *"the path can be cleared"* by providing practical guidance and tweaking the environment, HR can be more successful in driving business results.

HR Levers

The research and best practices presented in Part One of *Fearless HR* shows that HR impacts the business in many ways. While there can be other reasons for these outcomes, talent practices are a significant contributor. So there are connections to explore and exploit in HR's relationship to driving business results.

These connections can be visualized through the metaphor of levers that can be manipulated in a system of connected parts. A lever is actually one of six simple machines that use mechanical advantage to magnify a force. Levers can be moved up or down. They can adjust the flow of new material into the system. They are also controllable and allow for *"dialing up and dialing back,"* depending on the situation. A business is similar to a complex system with many interacting parts; and HR has many levers that can be manipulated to drive this system to produce results.

At the broadest level, HR has three levers to drive business results. These levers are not discrete as a single initiative can deploy two or three levers to varying degrees. In fact, the most powerful initiatives should employ all three.

- **Strategic Alignment:** This lever pertains to the ability to execute the company's strategy and business goals. If the workforce is not aligned to the right strategic direction and business goals, there is little chance the strategy will be properly executed. The lack of alignment threatens future strength, competitive advantage and sustainability. Typically, an organization out of alignment—just like an old car—wobbles, flounders, is not efficient, and hard to steer.

- **Cost Savings:** HR can improve the profitability of the business by leading initiatives that reduce costs. These savings to the *bottom line* are usually immediate and direct; and because the people cost in a company is so large, the cost savings often involve reductions in staff or reductions in benefits. But cost savings can also occur from process improvements, use of effective technology, and more efficient and effective workplace practices. For example, a more effective recruiting process or on-boarding program reduces costs and adds productivity, without reducing staff.

It should also be noted that Cost Savings only go so far. Profit is certainly improved in the short term, but cost cutting does not lead to enduring success, innovation and future growth. An organization cannot cost cut its way to greatness.

- **Productivity Improvements:** HR can grow the top line of the business through its ability to be a force multiplier and implement effective—not just efficient—talent practices. While cost savings are usually realized immediately, productivity improvement often appear over a longer time period. This time delay is, of course, one of the reasons why CEOs emphasize cost savings.

  While cost savings and process improvements continue to be significant, HR professionals today must shape the organization and create the context in which talent and innovation flourish. The Productivity Improvement lever must be exercised.

> *"The amount a firm can save by reducing inefficiencies in HR processes is usually insignificant compared to the amount it can gain by building a more talented and engaged workforce."*
>
> *Steven Director, 2013*

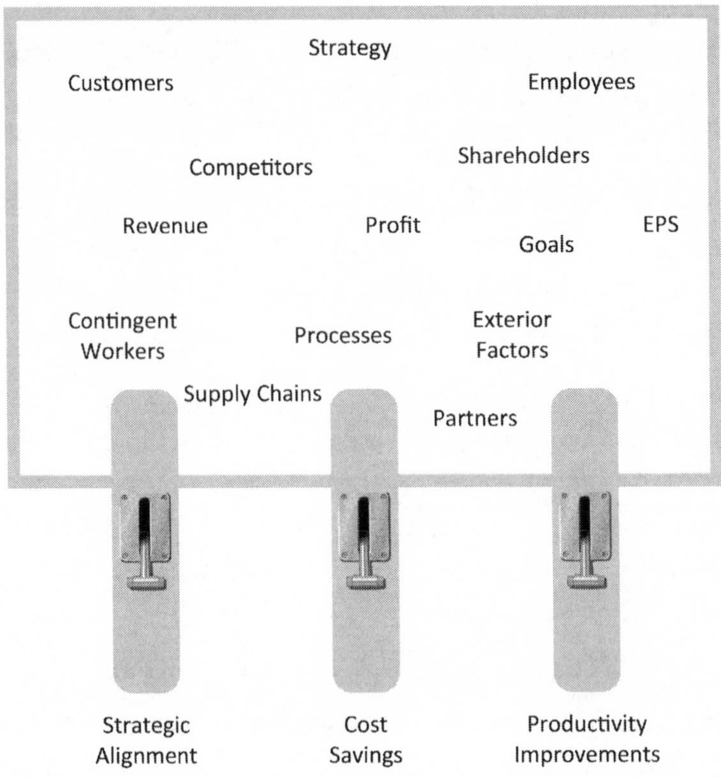

Figure 8-1: Levers in the Business Ecosystem

The Strategic Alignment Lever

There are three types of alignment that can be strengthened. The first is *employee alignment* and this pertains to the *"line of sight"* that an individual employee has to the strategy, business goals and values of the organization. If this line of sight is clear, employees understand their place in the organization and are more engaged. If the line of sight is murky or not apparent, then employees are more likely to be less connected and committed.

The second type of alignment focuses not on individual employees but the workforce as a whole. *Workforce alignment* is about optimizing and leveraging human capital resources to best execute strategy. The 6Rs (or the Jim Collin's metaphor of the bus) is the model most often used to describe the best fit between talent and executing strategy. Another often cited workforce alignment question is: are our best people doing the most important jobs?

The third type of alignment is *departmental alignment,* and this ensures that department goals and strategy are consistent and that departmental goals have been properly cascaded down the organization.

Figure 8-2 presents the different types of strategic alignment. The column entitled *"Types of Possible Savings/Benefits"* is intended to offer suggestions on measures that might be used in creating a business case. There are certainly other measures that could be used, but these can perhaps *kickstart* the process. The measure for *"the speed of trust"* is taken from Covey's work that says that business processes can occur from three to five times faster in high-trust environments. It also speaks to the shared cultural values that enable governance to occur more efficiently and effectively than relying on external rules and regulations (Seidman, 2008).

Category	**Focus**	**Types of Possible Savings/Benefits**
Employee Alignment	Strategic Line of Sight.	50% of employees do not know what is expected of them at work (Gallup). Less than 20% of change initiatives achieve their goals (Kotter). Engagement is higher for strong alignment.
Employment Alignment	Values/Culture Line of Sight	Actively disengaged employees cost the company $3400 for every $10K in combined salary. Engagement is higher for strong alignment. The speed of trust (Covey).
Workforce Alignment	The 6Rs: Right job, people, skills, time, place and cost	Poor execution. Not having best performers in most critical roles. Excellent performers outperform their peers by 5X.
Workforce Alignment	The 7Bs: Build, buy, borrow, boost, bounce, bind, balance.	Spending too much or too little on the workforce. Key positions unfilled: $7000/day. Loss of intellectual capital.
Departmental Alignment	Strategic Cascade	Only 10% of strategies are successfully implemented (Norton). Less than 20% of change initiatives achieve their goals (Kotter).
Departmental Alignment	Values/Culture Cascade	Engagement is higher for strong alignment. The speed of trust (Covey).

Figure 8-2: The Strategic Alignment Lever

THE COST SAVINGS LEVER

HR is most often associated with cost reductions, and furthermore with the cost reductions linked to layoffs, re-organizations and eliminating valued programs. While this is understandable because these savings are usually immediate and direct; it is also an incomplete picture. An organization can become more efficient in a number of ways, including lean six sigma process improvements, first time quality programs, better system design, improved policies, a different mix of resources and more powerful technologies.

The examples in Figure 8-3 are meant to be illustrative of the range of efficiencies that can result from the Cost Savings Lever. Continue to work with and add to this list of practical ways in which HR can drive business results through cost savings.

Category	Situation	Types of Possible Savings/Benefits
Hiring Process	Open requisitions	The organization is running at reduced efficiency.
Hiring Process	Cost to hire	Monetized savings from fewer external agencies.
Hiring Process	Time to hire	Reduction in time to fill resulting in less hiring manager and recruiter's time.
On-boarding	Time to proficiency	Faster rise to full productivity. Monetize the weeks savings (salary) in a shorter time to proficiency.
L and D Process	Shorter training programs and less use of classrooms	Cost savings from fewer facilities, and less instructor and delegate travel and expenses.
Staffing Levels	Span of control	Quantify savings for fewer managers.
Staffing Levels	Optimum staffing and borrowed talent levels	Compare costs before and after streamlined operations. Recognize the premium paid for ongoing *"borrowed"* talent.
Global Operations	Local vs foreign national hires	On average, expatriate costs are 3 to 5 times greater than local nationals.
Global Operations	Span of control	Compare savings for short term versus long term assignments.
Regrettable Turnover	Turnover within the first two years	1.5 times fully burdened salary for unwanted turnover
Regrettable Turnover	Turnover of high performers	Higher performers are worth 3 to 5 times the contributions of capable employees.
Benefits-Compensation Mix	New health care program	Document reduced health care costs.
Benefits-Compensation Mix	New retirement program	Document reduced pension expenses.
Wastage	Cost of errors	Rework costs
Wastage	Shrinkage	Costs for disappearing goods and materials.
Technology Efficiencies	Implementing new technologies	Reduction in duplicate maintenance costs, improvement in data entry costs, less IT support.
Facilities	Reduced footprint	Flexible work arrangements.
Organizational Design	Integration of talent practices	Fewer redundancies and less wasted time between functional handoffs.

Figure 8-3: Cost Savings from More Efficient and Different HR Initiatives

THE PRODUCTIVITY IMPROVEMENT LEVER

The Productivity Improvement Lever is the longer play. Productivity impacts are not as immediately apparent as cost reductions, but ultimately productivity gains are more important because they are the key to long term growth, innovation and sustainability.

It is more difficult to develop a business case for productivity improvements than for cost reductions. But it would be abrogating HR's role to drive business results if the Productivity Improvement Lever were not employed. It is through these actions that HR becomes the force multiplier and thinks a lead time ahead. It is through these actions that innovation occurs and talent flourishes; and it is through these actions that HR leaders become respected and trusted business leaders.

Again, the examples in Figure 8-4 are meant to be illustrative of the range of effective practices that can result from the Productivity Improvement Lever. Notice that this list is approximately twice as long as the Cost Savings list. Continue to work with and add to this list of practical ways in which HR can drive business results by improving productivity and the top line..

Category	Situation	Types of Possible Savings/ Benefits
Workforce Planning	Capability development	Staffing is at the right level and the workforce has the skills to be successful now. The risk is missed opportunity, extended deadlines and poor quality work.
Workforce Planning	Planning for future scenarios	Reduce risk that could impact future performance and competitiveness by 10%.
Succession Planning	Ready-now leadership pipeline	Costs for not having leaders ready now to fill vacant positions is equivalent to 3X the leader's fully burdened salary.
Succession Planning	Leadership build-buy ratio	40% of external leadership new hires fail within 18 months. Usually the ideal balance is 80% internal to 20% external.
Succession Planning	Ready-now strategic role pipeline	Costs for operating without a key player can be $7000 per day.
Talent Acquisition	Attracting top talent	The value of top performers is 2 to 4 times the value provided by competent performers.

Category	Situation	Types of Possible Savings/ Benefits
Talent Acquisition	Quality of hire	Quality hiring sources are two to three times more likely to yield high performers.
Deployment	Learning zone assignments	Related to improved engagement and continuing to keep people challenged.
Deployment	Internal mobility	Compares breakeven point for internal versus external hires; internal hires are already familiar with the culture.
Development	On-boarding break-even point	Contributes value faster by being productive sooner. Calculate time saved and multiply by pro-rated salary and benefits.
Development	Social capital network growth	People with larger professional networks are more productive by approximately 10%.
Development	Quality development programs	Leads to improved sales, customer loyalty and employee productivity.
Engagement	Workforce engagement	Engaged employees are more productive, more innovative and their efforts lead to increased sales and profitability.
Engagement	High potential/ performance engagement	Up to 10% of an organization's performance can be attributed to employee engagement.
Leadership	Leader effectiveness through engagement and 360 surveys	Leaders have a significant impact on engagement.
Leadership	Leaders teaching leaders	Related to more effective learning programs and stronger engagement.
Management	Manager effectiveness through engagement and 360 surveys	40% of managers are ineffective and cost the organization roughly 10X salary.
Management	Communication/ engagement programs	15 of the top 20 drivers of engagement are manager-related so the manager role is crucial.
Recognition	High impact recognition programs	Six fold increase in operating margin for organizations that recognize excellence.
Collaboration	Community building activities	Contributes to expanding professional networks, a greater sense of community and faster/better decision making.

Category	Situation	Types of Possible Savings/ Benefits
Collaboration	Cross-functional assignments	Mitigates risk by having more employees who are cross-trained and multifunctional. This can also result in fewer hires.
Innovation	Number of innovations	Compare the number/types of new products over the past years, especially from ground-up innovation programs.
Innovation	Revenue impact of innovations	Calculate the percentage of revenue coming from new products each year.
Quality	Rework percentage	Additional revenue from fewer quality correction costs after training and coaching.
Quality	Customer net promoter score	Greatest source of revenue and profits is customer loyalty. Correlated with high employee engagement benefits.
Operational Productivity	Throughput	Faster build time because of better skills and processes.
Operational Productivity	Supply chain output	Improved performance from suppliers and partners.
Culture	Governance system	Faster and better decision making. Lack of trust increases the cost of doing business up to six times.
Culture	Reinforcing employment brand	Related to attracting top talent, sustainable engagement and turnover within the first two years.

Figure 8-4: Increased Revenues from Improved Productivity and More Effective HR Practices

Taking Action to Select the Right HR Levers

Almost fifty practical examples of improved business results from HR Levers have been identified in Figures 8-2, 3 and 4. But now the question becomes which of these actions should be taken? The answer to this question is dependent on the strategy and health of the business. As business leaders, HR professionals should always be trying to improve business results, but some initiatives are more impactful than others. Time and resources are, of course, limited, so how are decisions made and priorities established? While conditions will always vary, there are several guidelines that can assist in the selection of the right HR Levers to select.

Guideline 1. Strategic and Business Importance. There must be a direct link from the initiative to the organization's strategy, strategic initiatives and/or business goals. It should be possible to array all the possible actions and initiatives in terms of their strategic fit and urgency, with some scoring higher than others. This guideline can weed out initiatives that are a good idea or a personal agenda, but not essential to the success of the business.

Guideline 2. Magnitude of Savings and Improvements Over Time. Some initiatives will yield greater results than others, and presumably the initiatives that produce the most value/money should be prioritized higher. The factor of time must also be considered as some benefits may take too long to be realized; and therefore a smaller savings that is achieved faster may be elevated to a higher priority. (Please refer to the next section on *Estimating the Magnitude of Benefits and Justifying HR Initiatives* for a step-by-step treatment of how to monetize savings and improvements).

Guideline 3. Execution Parameters. Some initiatives are harder to implement than others, and this factor should be part of the prioritization process. A project, for example, can have excellent financial benefits, but simply may be too difficult to accomplish within existing time and resource constraints. One useful technique is to weigh the difference between the current state and future state of a proposed change. If the gap is small, then execution is easier than an initiative that is disruptive and radically changes the workplace.

Guideline 4. Balance of Levers. HR is too often just associated with cost reduction through personnel actions. While reducing *"people"* costs is often a significant source of savings; there are other avenues to improve the business. Think beyond the short term, have a balance of short and longer term initiatives, and include all three levers (strategic alignment, cost savings and productivity improvements) to drive business results.

Guideline 5. Tipping Point: Number of Concurrent Change Initiatives. How much change can an organization sustain? This question is difficult to answer in the abstract without knowing other information, most notably the strategic importance and execution parameters. But there is certainly wisdom in not trying to do too many things at the same time, because the risk is that everything will be *"half-baked."* Especially given time, focus and resource limitations, trying to implement more than two or three large impact change initiatives at once is problematic.

Estimating the Magnitude of Benefits and Justifying HR Initiatives

An important part of the action plan in the previous section is the estimation of the expected savings and improvements (Guideline 2). These benefits typically come from an investment, action or initiative that is taken to address a business situation. Actions, such as a reduction in force or removing a pension benefit, usually do not require an investment for the savings to occur. But often with productivity improvements, an initiative is required to drive the savings and productivity gains. For example, a new onboarding program drives improved productivity by shortening the learning curve. This new onboarding program, however, costs money; and it is reasonable for the organization to question the return on this investment. Organizations have many requests for money, and not all projects can or should be funded.

Capital Budgeting Models in finance compare different investments an organization can make. These investments can include equipment, business expansions, acquisitions, technology, and HR programs, such as the aforementioned onboarding program, recognition incentives, new training courses and recruiting platforms. *Capital investments* are expected to have a return on the invested capital, while *ordinary expenditures,* such as supplies and utilities, are not.

A set of steps can be used to evaluate capital HR investments. These HR projects cost money, and the question becomes: Is this project a good investment for the company or can greater returns be gained elsewhere? The cost justification of HR initiatives becomes an important skill for HR professionals to possess, as it combines business acumen, financial literacy, influencing skills and change management.

Cost Justification of HR Initiatives

Step 1. Specify the HR project. This step provides the answer to the question: what is proposed?

Step 2. Define the business issue that the HR initiative addresses. This seems simple to do, but it may be more complex than anticipated. Getting to the root cause of the business problem as opposed to symptoms is the dilemma. Use lean techniques such as *"The Five Whys"* to continue to probe for the real business issue. This step provides the *why* behind the what (the initiative).

Step 3. Identify the primary stakeholders and audiences impacted by the HR initiative. It is very easy to forget key stakeholders, and when this happens, the project is at risk. It is also insufficient just to list the audiences and stakeholders; identify the key concerns for each group and their likely support for the project. It is very useful to understand the type of evidence and presentation that is most compelling for each key player.

Step 4. Determine the Barriers and Possible Unintended Outcomes. Before proceeding to the actual business case, it is best to describe the potential issues that could arise from the HR initiative. Because the business case will be built on the positive aspects of the initiative, it is very possible that *unintended* consequences may arise; and these consequences may be important to key stakeholders.

Step 5. Determine the *Cash Outlay* for the project. How much does this initiative cost? Remember to think through all cost categories such as product, installation, maintenance and updates. Also, identify the life cycle of the project and allocate costs to the appropriate year. Work with a financial buddy to determine if depreciation should be applied over the life cycle of the investment.

Step 6. Project *Future Cash Inflows* from the investment. What are the expected returns for making this investment? In this step, the key benefits are monetized so that costs can subsequently be compared to revenues. The recommended process to follow is:

- Brainstorm all potential benefits for the investment, regardless if the they can be monetized or not.
- Prioritize the total list of benefits by importance and ease of monetization.
- Select two to four benefits to monetize, but keep the others to include in the final presentation. It is usually easier to monetize benefits that reduce costs as opposed to those that increase productivity. In selecting the two to four benefits, it is important to know the benefits that are most important to key sponsors and stakeholders.

An example: Replacing a two-week classroom-based training program on customer service skills with e-learning courses that can be completed in one week. The e-learning programs can be completed at a person's desktop and can be accessed and completed at any time (asynchronous training).

This is an actual example of an HR initiative, and the project team followed the steps for justifying the cost for the e-learning courses. A series of benefits were listed by the project team and some were selected to monetize for the business case.

Benefits for the e-learning Solution	Priority for Monetization	Formula
Consistent approach: everyone receives the same training	Low	
Greater accountability and improved tracking of test scores and completion	Low	
Productivity savings as e-learning takes half the time	High	Calculate one week of productivity savings by either pro-rating the average yearly salary or the cost of a replacement project worker for one week; and then multiply by the number of students.
Eliminates student travel costs because e-learning courses can be taken in the workplace	High	Estimate travel and living costs and multiply by the number of students. At $400 per day, for example, for 10 days (2 weeks), this cost adds up very quickly.
Eliminates instructor and room rental fees	High	Estimate instructor and room costs for 10 days.
Easier to update and maintain	Low	
Greater student interactions and participation	Low	

Figure 8-5: Benefits for an e-Learning Customer Service Training Solution

The business case for the e-learning program expense was made by monetizing three benefits: one week of productivity gains, eliminating student travel costs and eliminating recurring instructor and facility costs. The payback period was less than 18 months and the Internal Rate of Return (see following discussion) was greater than 35%. But interestingly, in the final presentation of the business case, the biggest benefit for the *Vice President of Customer Service* was greater accountability and tracking so she could know with certainty *"who did what."* This is a benefit that essentially comes for free as the business case was strong enough based on other factors. It is valuable then to present all benefits, not just those that are monetized.

Step 7. Compare the Costs and Anticipated Revenues by the following methods:

- *Payback Period.* The amount of time to get your money back. If the payback period is longer than the life cycle of the project, there is no reason to make the investment. Also, depending on the financial condition of a company, it may not want to consider an investment with a payback period of longer, for example, than three years.
- *Net Present Value (NPV):* This analysis takes into account the time value of money (which the payback period does not) and is usually the finance professional's first choice for analyzing capital expenditures. NPV can be calculated through standard spreadsheet functionality, but essentially any investment with an NPV greater than 0 means that the proposed investment is earning more than the company's hurdle rate (what it could get from investing the money).
- *Internal Rate of Return:* This method allows for direct comparison of the return rate for the project to the company's hurdle rate. If a company has a hurdle rate of 10%, this means that they won't consider an investment lower than 10%. If the project has an internal rate of return of 15%, then this is a good use of company money. It still doesn't mean that the investment will be made, because there are competing priorities to possibly consider.

Step 8. Other Financial Factors. There may be other capital budgeting factors to consider and these would be known by colleagues in Finance. It is always best to create or at least validate the business case with a finance buddy.

Step 9. Make a Compelling Case. The final presentation of the HR cost justification should be developed with the audience in mind. Is it a presentation to several executives or just the CHRO? Has a time limit been set for the presentation? Have all stakeholders been identified? Here are several guidelines for effective executive presentations.

- Tailor the presentation to your audience. Know the type of evidence that is most meaningful to key players in the audience.
- Use business language, not *"HR speak."*
- Practice the presentation to ensure that the timing and flow are effective.
- Establish a strong connection in the first 60 to 90 seconds.
- Reinforce the burning platform and why change is necessary: *the why behind the what.*
- BLUF: bottom line up front and be clear about the main points to convey.
- Employ high production values by eliminating errors, consistent use of fonts and sizing, using visuals to reinforce key points, having tag lines for emphasis and eliminating overly busy slides.
- End strongly. Be clear about *"the ask."* End the presentation by asking for a commitment and recommendations.

HR has many levers it can manipulate to drive business results. Business results improve when strategic alignment is stronger, costs are reduced and revenue grows. HR has a direct impact on all three avenues. And despite popular opinion, these business results can be monetized and presented to executives, just as any capital improvement might be. Now, let's look at a set of five tools that apply several of the concepts in this treatment of *"Implementing the Right HR Levers."*

Tools and Templates

Tool 1: Strategy Alignment Framework

This is a great tool to check the alignment of HR projects/actions with strategy and strategic initiatives; and then to link the HR project to measures and business outcomes. This tool continues to stress the value of HR being anchored in strategy and then being a more data-driven and evidenced-based discipline.

Strategy	HR Project	Measures	Outcomes

Tool 2: Intended and Unintended Outcomes for HR Projects

It is important to be able to articulate both the intended and unintended possible consequences of an HR project or action. This tool provides a strategic, longer term view of HR projects beyond just the immediate and obvious impacts. The Unintended Outcomes can often be overlooked, but may be real threats or risks to the project. Consider the example of outsourcing an HR function. Unintended outcomes might be 1) loss of morale for remaining employees; 2) a possible drop in quality, and 3) loss of integration with other HR functions. It is best to understand these possible risks and address them before they become major problems.

HR Project	Intended Outcomes	Unintended Outcomes

Tool 3: HR Lever Prioritization Scheme

This scheme provides a basis for making decisions about which HR Levers are the highest priority. Organizations have limited resources, money and attention spans. HR professionals are also busy and have to pick the best battles to fight. Too much change at any one time can be debilitating, so the right choices have to be made. This tool identifies the major factors to be considered and weighed.

HR Project/Action	Strategic and Business Importance	Magnitude of Savings and Improvements	Execution Parameters	Balance of Levers	Tipping Point

Tool 4: Financial Business Case Framework

The major elements of a financial business case are included in this tool. The listing of potential benefits should include those that are difficult to monetize, because these benefits may be particularly important to key stakeholders. From this list of potential benefits, select two or four that can be monetized for the business case. As discussed, it is useful to complete the business case with a colleague in the financial organization.

HR Project	Cost	Potential Benefits	Benefits to Monetize	Payback Period and ROI

Tool 5: Historical Review of Driving Business Results

HR professionals need to build their own legacy. By charting major initiatives and projects, and the savings and improvements they produced; HR can have better evidence on its impact and outcomes. It is easy to forget what past projects have accomplished and how HR can drive the business. This tool documents the many ways that HR can drive and improve the business over time.

HR Project/Action	Timeframe	Cost Saving	Productivity Improvements	Lessons Learned

SUMMARY

HR is the one function that touches every person in the organization, and with the right talent, capabilities and professional networks, HR professionals can and do drive business results.

But no matter how ready and capable HR professionals are, they may still wonder what can HR actually do to impact the business. A system of HR Levers has been proposed that seeks to strengthen internal alignment, cost savings and productivity improvements. HR is often associated with just one type of cost savings—internal staff reductions. But there are many other ways in which both the top and bottom line business results can be strengthened. HR professionals certainly recognize the value needed short term cost savings, but they must also look longer term to insure that the workplace enables talent to flourish, innovation to occur and the company to grow.

Fifty different examples of HR Levers have been described, and these examples *"clear the path."* They demonstrate what can be done. The determination of which ones are relevant to a particular organization is based on a prioritization scheme that includes Strategic and Business Importance, the Magnitude of Savings, and Execution Parameters. There is also a Tipping Point, after which too much change can breed uncertainty and confusion. It is now time to address the final opportunity for HR to be a driver of business results.

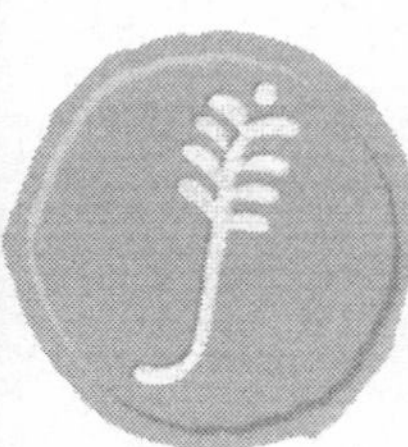

Chapter 9

Demonstrating a *Fearless* Mindset

> *"Be the change that you want to see in the world."*
>
> *Mahatma Gandhi*

With all of the perceptions and stereotypes that have dogged HR over the years, there is little wonder that the profession has a confidence problem. *Fearless HR* has addressed five of these myths in Part 1:

- HR Does Not Add Value to the Business
- HR is Siloed and Too Inwardly Focused
- HR is a Weak Discipline with Poor Tools
- HR Measures are Too Soft and Subjective
- HR is a Stodgy, Dead-end Career

While evidence has been presented to counter the current relevancy of these historical perceptions, it can take years if not decades for views to change. And views do not change with a single presentation, research study or breakthrough article. It takes an accumulated wealth of evidence to counter beliefs, and then the message must be continual. In advertising, there is a Rule of 10 that stipulates that the key message must be said over and over, using a variety of media and methods, before the message *"sticks."*

Part Two of *Fearless HR* presents the opportunities for HR to drive business results. Four specific opportunities are delineated, and their order is relevant. First, HR professionals must get better through strengthening their capabilities and enhancing their professional network. These steps improve skills and unlock the tacit knowledge of colleagues through meaningful connections and conversations. Second, there needs to be practical examples of how HR can actually drive business results. These illustrative examples taken from a variety of organizations—big and small—can help clear the path for the three HR Levers: Strategic Alignment, Cost Savings and Productivity Improvements.

While these are necessary steps for HR to drive business results, they are not sufficient by themselves. The missing ingredient is the spirit to escape past perceptions, to take risks and to advance the business. This needed ingredient is a bold mindset, resolute point of view and professional confidence. It is important that this new mindset be demonstrated ***after*** capabilities have been improved and the path has been cleared. A *Fearless Mindset* without being able to deliver the *"goods"* is premature and can be detrimental. HR professionals have to be able to deliver on promises and expectations; unwarranted confidence damages trust and threatens HR's ability to drive business results.

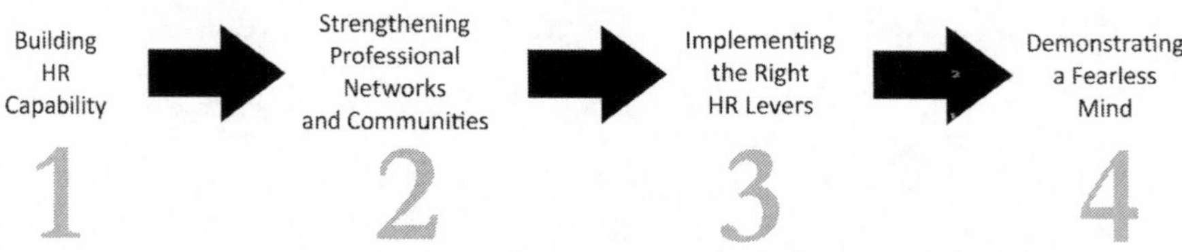

Figure 9-1: The Proper Sequence for HR Opportunities

We have seen the downside of mindsets built on negative perceptions of a profession. There is thankfully a corollary. Mindsets can be built on positive perceptions as well. The new positive mindset is that **HR drives business results, and to accomplish this goal, HR must be fearless.** It must not be a silent partner or a tentative player. With this confidence and positive mindset—together with the skills and colleagues to deliver the goods and a path made clearer by practical examples—HR can achieve its new aspirations and make significant contributions to the health and strength of the business. Mindsets, do indeed matter, and are key to the future efficacy of HR.

RESEARCH AND THOUGHT LEADERSHIP ON MINDSET

There is a growing body of research and inquiry on the power of mindsets. As we have seen, mindsets can open up new possibilities or they can shortcut reality and reduce our vision. Whether the perceptions are negative or positive, mindsets certainly influence subsequent behavior. Carol Dweck, a leading expert in the power of mindsets, describes the focus of her inquiry.

> *My work is part of a tradition in psychology that shows the power of people's beliefs. These may be beliefs we're aware of or unaware of, but they strongly affect what we want and whether we succeed in getting it. This tradition also shows how changing people's beliefs—even the simplest beliefs—can have profound effects.*
>
> *Carol Dweck, Mindset: The New Psychology of Success, 2006*

Five different lines of inquiry focus on the power and impact of mindsets. They are:

- Carol Dweck on fixed and growth mindsets.
- The Pygmalion stories and studies on the power of self-filling prophecies.
- Robert Sutton and Huggy Rao on *Scaling Up Excellence* (2014).
- Blue and Red Oceans
- Neuroscience on bias and stereotyping

1. Dweck on Mindsets.

Carol Dweck has studied mindsets for more than two decades. She has found that people have one of two mindsets about their personal abilities and skills, and that these beliefs have a profound impact on their life. People with a *Fixed Mindset* believe that their qualities are carved in stone. You have inherited a set of skills and abilities, and this is the hand you are dealt. People with a *Growth Mindset* think that their qualities can be developed and grown through experience and application. They believe that a person's true potential is unknown and can be shaped by "passion, toil and training."

Theses distinctions are not new, and there is a lot of folklore around these two belief systems. The *nature versus nurture* debate is certainly similar in many respects. But Dweck takes the two mindsets and demonstrates how they impact thoughts, actions, views about learning and effort, and definitions of success and failure. Furthermore, these actions play out in school, sports, the workplace and relationships.

One simple example of how the two mindsets play out in life is to study people's ability to assess their own strengths and weaknesses. Many studies have shown that people are not good at estimating their own abilities and performance (hence 180° and 360° surveys). But when further investigation is done, almost all of the inaccuracies come from people that have *Fixed Mindsets*. People with *Growth Mindsets* are actually quite proficient diagnosing themselves, probably because they are committed to getting better.

There are two applications of Dweck's research and analysis for *Fearless HR*. First, it is very clear that mindsets do matter and that they lead to subsequent actions and behaviors. If people hold negative perceptions of HR—whether the five historical perceptions treated earlier or others—those assumptions and views should be surfaced and challenged. If these beliefs are ignored or go unchallenged, they will endure and inhibit HR's future. The path to the future can only cleared when the past is reconciled.

The second lesson from Dweck's work is that HR professionals need to embrace the *Growth Mindset* and the learning, challenge, effort and passion it includes. There is simply no room for a *Fixed Mindset* in a rapidly changing world in which collaboration, networks and connections are so crucial to success.

2. The Pygmalion Stories and Studies.

Eliza Doolittle, one of the most beloved theater characters of all time, reminds us that the difference between a flower girl and a lady is not how she behaves, but how she is perceived and treated. And when Professor Higgins changes his perspective, he sees things very differently. The flower girl becomes the lady. The Pygmalion story is a powerful parable about self-fulfilling prophecies.

It turns out that this effect transcends myth. A series of studies examined this effect in both the classroom and the workplace. Rosenthal and Jacobsen (1968) conducted an experiment in which teachers were given a list of 20% of elementary school students who showed significant potential to blossom within the year. Unbeknown to the teachers, this list was actually randomly generated and the 20% group was no different than the larger student population. Returning eight months later, the 20% group significantly outperformed their peers. While the Rosenthal and Jacobsen research has been criticized by some, its basic findings have been replicated in both educational and business contexts, and are now engrained at least in folklore and public consciousness.

At the core of these studies is that expectations somehow get translated to others, probably subconsciously, and these expectations become true. The teachers, for example, in the original study never addressed the 20% sample with words such as "OK, smart kids, let's do this." But perhaps through body language, pacing, informal words of encouragement or reinforcement activities, expectations do get transferred to behavior in some way, shape or form and do become self-fulfilling prophecies. This transference occurs for both positive and negative expectations, called subsequently the Rosenthal effect for positive expectations leading to positive performance and its corollary, the Golem effect for negative expectations and resulting behavior.

Within business contexts, there are positive correlations between leader expectations and follower performance. J. Stirling Livingston authored an article for the Harvard Business Review in 1969 entitled simply "Pygmalion in Management." Among his observations:

- What managers expect of subordinates and the way they treat them largely determine their performance and career progress.
- A unique characteristic of superior managers is the ability to create high performance expectations that subordinates fulfill.
- Less effective managers fail to develop similar expectations, and as a consequence, the productivity of their subordinates suffers.

- Subordinates, more often than not, appear to do what they believe they are expected to do.

The lessons from the Pygmalion stories and studies are that mindsets do find a way to shape behavior, and that unless mindsets are addressed, behavior is unlikely to change. As modern HR professionals, our actions, confidence and expectations are vital, not just for ourselves, but for colleagues as well. Remember the Contagion Effect in the discussion of professional networks; attitudes and beliefs do get conveyed, intended or not. If we are not committed to the belief that HR drives business results, then others will doubt HR's contributions as well.

3. Sutton and Rao on "Scaling Excellence: Getting to More without Settling for Less." In a wide ranging study on the difficulty of spreading constructive beliefs and behavior from the few to the many, the authors propose ideas that have a direct bearing on changing HR's mindset. These ideas come from their experience teaching a course on "Scaling Excellence" at Stanford and from their experiences working with many leading companies around the world. Among their insights:

- **Spread a Mindset, Not Just a Footprint.** Here is that "Mindset" word again. The authors state that *"effective scaling depends on believing and living a shared mindset throughout your group, division or organization. It requires stating the beliefs and living the behavior, and then doing it again and again. These shared convictions reduce confusion, disagreements and unnecessary dead-ends—and diminish the chance that excellence will fade as your footprint expands."* For HR to change, it must be able to articulate, live and transfer that change to others.

- **Engage All the Senses:** Bolster mindset with supportive sights, sounds and cues that others may barely notice at all. In an interesting array of studies, the authors emphasize that the environment can be changed to support a mindset by introducing a number of subtle, almost imperceptible changes. They talk about Starbucks recovering its momentum in 2007 by among other practices getting back to core values and customers again smelling freshly ground coffee; or of Disney's cast members who bend down to talk to children on their level or are always in-character by never talking on a cell phone or chewing gum.

- **Accelerate Accountability.** People have to own the mindset and accompanying change. If they feel detached or disjointed, it is easy to disavow ownership. If they feel it is someone else's responsibility, then it will be no one's responsibility.

> *"Accountability means that an organization is packed with people who embody and protect excellence, who work vigorously to spread it to others, and spot, help, critique and (when necessary) push aside colleagues who fail to live and spread it."*
>
> *Sutton and Rao, 2015*

4. Blue and Red Oceans. One of the best-selling business books of all time is *Blue Ocean Strategies* (2005) by W. Chan Kim and Renee Mauborgne of INSEAD. The authors argue that instead of attempting to fight competitors in crowded marketplaces (i.e., red oceans), the greatest value is achieved through creating blue oceans of uncontested market spaces. In blue oceans, the marketplace is unknown, demand is created not fought over, and there is ample opportunity for growth that is both rapid and profitable. Apple, of course, is the best example of a company that has created new industries where there were none, and accordingly is the most valued brand in the world. Cirque de Soliel is another example of a "Blue Ocean" by blending the circus art form with ballet and opera, while eliminating typical circus actors such as star performers and tamed wild animals.

Kim and Mauborgne (2015) have further extended their core principles in an Harvard Business Review article entitled *"Red Ocean Traps."* In this article they talk about the mental models that cause people to fall back on old notions of competition and restrict implementing blue ocean strategies, even though all the data says they should. By mental models, they mean:

> *"ingrained assumptions and theories about the way the world works. Though mental models lie below people's cognitive awareness, they're so powerful a determinant of choices and behaviors that many neuroscientists think of them almost as automated algorithms that dictate how people respond to changes and events.*
>
> *Kim and Mauborgne, 2015*

While acknowledging that mental models do have their merits, they also inhibit managers and leaders from breaking away from traditions, relying on old patterns, and not seeing the new reality.

There are several implications of Kim and Mauborgne's research for HR professionals. First, as is evidenced by others, mindsets and mental models are powerful determinants of behavior. If these beliefs are at odds with current facts, evidence and direction; then they should be addressed, challenged and corrected. Second, as HR professionals become recognized as business leaders, they must take a longer term view, see the bigger picture and embrace blue ocean thinking as a potential fertile landscape for improving business results.

And the third lesson is the actions taken by the authors themselves. They have devoted their life's work to a well-respected theory—Blue Ocean Strategies—and yet it has not been as widely practiced as they hoped. Instead of sulking, being disappointed or just dropping out, they endeavored to study the problem, find out why and propose solutions. They understand that it is not unusual at all for a theory that challenges past convention to take time and patience before it is widely accepted.

A similar type of perseverance has been demonstrated by Marcus Buckingham, one of the most respected researchers and thought leaders in talent practices and leadership. Buckingham was one of the original authors for the ground-breaking Gallup study *"First Break All the Rules"* which established the Q12 as standard for engagement studies. He then spent the next several decades of his career focusing on one of the twelve questions: *"At work, do I have the opportunity to do what I do best every day?"*

This seemingly simple question has opened up lengthy discussions on: strengths-based development, strengths-finder tools, positive psychology, positivity ratios, buoyancy, appreciative inquiry at the organizational level, and working with such respected figures as Donald Clifton and Jack Zenger. Buckingham's work posits that people (and managers) gain greater success by focusing on strengths first and not over emphasizing weaknesses that are not crucial. He uses the story of a child coming home with a report card to show how most people focus on weaknesses, not strengths. The child gives the report card to the parent and it contains the grades of: A, A-, A, B+, B+, B- and C+. Buckingham suggests that most of us will ask about the B- and C+ and not recognize the achievement that the A grades represent.

Buckingham cites multiple research studies that prove that the strengths-based approach is superior, but, again, practice lags and people revert to old ways and habits. While Buckingham may be personally disappointed that more headway has not been made in the strengths-based movement, he continues to trumpet the message in new and different ways. It is also interesting to speculate that perhaps the recent move to revamp the process of performance management may owe a debt to the work of Marcus Buckingham over the years.

The lesson from the perseverance of Kim, Mauborgne and Buckingham for HR professionals is that, often in spite of evidence, it takes a long time for behavioral patterns to change. There must, then, be a *continual case* for HR driving business results.

5. The Neuroscience of Bias and Stereotyping. Chris Bergonzi (2015) explores the topic of bias and stereotyping (negative Mindsets) in his article *"Exploring the Neural Pathways of Prejudice May Offer Clues to Lessening Its Impact."* Scientists distinguish between parts of the brain that immediately discern threats (amygdala) and the part that provides longer term conscious thought, judgments and semantic memory (cerebral cortex). Unconscious bias emanating from the amygdala is an immediate, reflexive and essentially a defensive reaction anchored in our survival instincts. The problem is that this "blink of the eye" reflex sets the stage for the cognitive components of social categorization, stereotypes, prejudices, and inequality. In other words, unconscious bias can cause creativity and higher order thinking to be short circuited.

Researchers, however, indicate that the human brain is malleable enough to overcome bias. The introduction of even subtle cues such as being exposed to more diverse environments, counter examples of implicit bias, and linking positive intentions to a targeted group can all have salubrious effects. The good news is that these are not hugely sophisticated interventions to counteract bias; but they need to occur or else the immediate response becomes even more engrained.

The implications of this neuroscience for developing bias to the HR professional is that the historical perceptions of HR we have discussed may well stem from a similar dichotomy of quick reaction and longer-term processing. But the real lesson is that there are ways to overcome these myths, and some techniques are not overly complex or costly. One step is for each HR professional to be a role model for what HR can become. This sets an example, elevates the status of the profession and demonstrates the right behaviors to colleagues. Another step is for HR leaders to take an active role teaching other leaders and employees. The HR leaders become not only the most visible role models, but they also take an active role in transmitting the values and behaviors of HR driving business results.

These, then, are different lines of inquiry regarding the power of mindsets to influence opinion and direct behavior. From leading researchers to Greek myths to best-selling strategists to neuroscientists, the message is quite similar: Mindsets matter. Negative mindsets are not irreversible; they can be altered if they are recognized and corrected when at odds with evidence and future direction. And there is extensive power in positive mindsets that set the stage for new futures, and in HR's case, driving business results and becoming a trusted and respected business leader.

> *"Whether you think you can or whether you think you can't, you are right."*
>
> *Henry Ford*

PURPOSE FUELS MINDSET

A positive mindset, such as *Fearless HR driving business results*, is accelerated by a strong and meaningful purpose. People want to be involved with companies and professions that are principled and stand for something beyond a paycheck or profits. They want to be associated with something larger than themselves and find meaning in their contributions. Artists and psychologists have understood this truth for years—some such as Victor Frankel under the most tragic of conditions. Chip Conley, author and ex-CEO of Joie de Vivre boutique hotels, brings Maslow to the workplace by stressing the value of providing not just jobs or careers for employees, but a *calling*. Dan Pink identifies intrinsic (not extrinsic) motivators as driving performance of complex work, and *purpose* is one of the three motivators he describes.

> *"Purpose comes when we know we have done something that we believe matters—to others, to society and to ourselves."*
>
> *Aaron Hurst, The Purpose Economy, 2014*

Organizations are now increasingly being evaluated on not one but multiple bottom lines. This idea was first articulated as the triple bottom line (3BL) by John Elkington in 1994; and has now gone mainstream, especially after the avarice of Enron, WorldCom, Tyco, Lehman Brothers, AIG, and others that artificially inflated earnings and the bottom line without concern for laws, ethics or others beyond themselves. Rosabeth Moss Kanter (2009) has talked about *Vanguard Companies*, in which high business performance and strong societal contributions are directly linked. Lauri Bassi and colleagues discuss the *"Era of Worthiness"* and companies that are good, will not just survive, but thrive. Dave and Wendy Ulrich introduce the term of *"Abundant Organizations"* that provide for meaning at work.

> *"The value of meaningful work that involves all of you….*
>
> 1. *Employees who find meaning at work are more competent, committed and contributing.*
> 2. *In turn, employee competence, commitment and sense of contribution lead to increased customer commitment.*
> 3. *In turn, customer commitment leads to better financial results for the company."*
>
> *Dave and Wendy Ulrich, The Why of Work, 2010*

Purpose is a meaningful motivator for all employees, not just millennials . Consider the example of Medtronic during Bill George's tenure as CEO. Each new employee received a medallion with the image of a sick person rising. He would then ask them:

> *"I ask in accepting this that you accept the mission of Medtronic and look at it and display it to remind you that the purpose of your being here is to restore people to full life and health. If you get frustrated, note that there is a higher calling."*
>
> *Bill George, past CEO Medtronic*

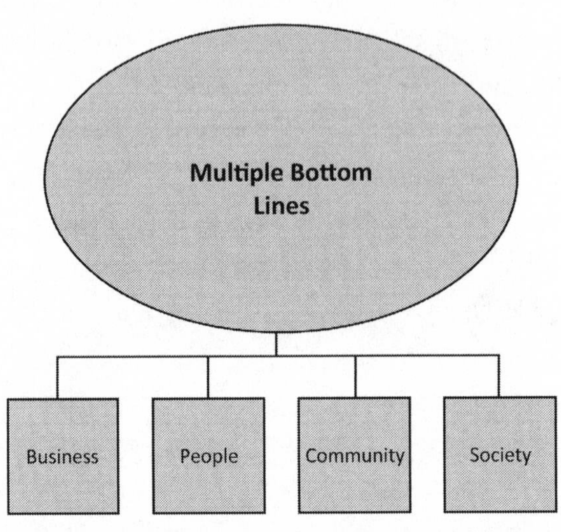

Figure 9-2: Multiple Bottom Lines

Even with organizations whose purpose is not as beneficial as saving lives, there are ways to craft meaning at work. Conley's boutique hotels, where many people clean rooms or put bills underneath doors in the early morning hours, the mantra to *"Create Joy"*—developed by the staff—binds everyone together. Purpose also may not be derived so much from what a business does, but *how* it does it. People are proud to work for an organization that makes ethical decisions and is principled; Proctor & Gamble and the Branson companies are just two examples of principles-based organizations.

Purpose is usually discussed in terms of organizations and companies, but it pertains to professions as well. The central question, then, becomes: *What is the purpose of HR?* The answers need to be more than just what HR does; it needs to address the *why* behind the *what.*

A personal observation:

Before writing this book, I started to think about the purpose of HR. I did this partially because so many writers whom I respect were raising the same issue, and partially because I was in front of hundreds of HR professionals at HCI courses or conferences and I wanted to feel as confident as possible in conveying the value of the HR profession.

So my conclusion was that I did, what I did, to help others improve their workplace and workforce. This phrase resonated for me, and it fueled me going to work every day and dealing with the distractions and requirements of any job…….dcf

HR has a major advantage in terms of purpose. While other functions have bonafide purposes, the HR function touches every person in the organization; and in the innovation economy, people are the greatest source of competitive advantage. *Fearless HR* advocates the broad purpose of HR driving business results through: 1) Creating the context in which talent and innovation can flourish, 2) Improving business results through better alignment, cost savings and productivity improvements, and 3) Becoming a trusted and effective business leader. This is a purpose that impacts the triple bottom line, affects people's aspirations and futures, and contributes not just to shareholders but citizens as well.

THE FEARLESS HR MINDSET

As a conclusion to both this chapter and Part II, let's review the qualities of Fearless HR leaders. Once the past perceptions that have constrained HR have been addressed, it is time to seize the opportunity for HR to drive business results. But this cannot happen with HR's current skill set; in fact, a number of things must happen for HR to make meaningful contributions to the business on a regular basis. For HR professionals, this change is not easy or quick to make; it takes dedicated and continual effort; just as it would for any professional who seeks to be at the top of his or her profession. In order for HR professionals to be respected and valued they need to be: improving their skills and abilities; adding to their experiences; broadening their professional networks; pulling the right levers; using data to make wiser decisions, becoming better business people; and then coaching others to enhance HR's new legacy of driving business results.

Figure 9-3 highlights the steps that need to be taken, not just to have a Fearless attitude, but to become a true business leader.

Fearless HR Qualities	Description
1. Becomes performance ready by improving capabilities and professional networks.	HR professionals must get better. You cannot drive results in a complex business environment with siloed perspectives and old skills. HR professionals must embrace continuous learning and the Growth Mindset (Dweck, 2006) in their constant search to improve. But "readiness" is not a casual statement; it must be a specific, data-driven and "crowd-sourced" condition. Readiness is not saying "I am all set now." It is using a systematic model such as The HR Capability Framework (Chapter 7), gathering data from peers on their view of skills, identifying specific developmental goals, and assessing their accomplishment. Readiness is hard work, and if steps are not taken to become ready to perform, HR leaders will miss a huge opportunity to drive business results.
2. Understands HR levers that impact the business.	There are many examples of the three HR Levers that drive business results through: 1) strategic alignment to the triple bottom line, 2) cost savings and 3) productivity improvements. It is important to recognize that HR is not simply about personnel reductions, there are many other levers than can and should be exercised to improve the top and bottom lines.
3. Believes in HR's purpose and creates a personalized, owned purpose.	A strong sense of purpose leads to professional confidence and accelerates the *Fearless HR* mindset. But as we have seen, a Fearless attitude is not sufficient by itself to drive business results: you have to have "the goods," take the right actions, and follow through before leadership is earned. Each person has a distinct *Owned Purpose* that particularly resonates with him or her.

Qualities	Description
4. Analyzes business problems using data, a systematic approach and communicates effectively.	These are expectations for any leader in the business. They encompass aspects of the HR Capability Framework, but these qualities have to be demonstrated consistently in the actual business environment. HR must be data driven and communicate in the language of the business.
5. Makes compelling and bold business cases.	When it is time to make recommendations and act, HR leaders do so with decisiveness, boldness and conviction. They have a strong point of view based on evidence, financial data and sound judgment, not bias or whim.
6. Is accountable for business results.	HR Leaders should be responsible for business results, not simply internal targets. Since they aspire to be business (not just HR) leaders, they should be held accountable to the same standard. Sharing business accountabilities with other leaders also builds connections and trust.
7. Seeks evidence to determine effectiveness of projects and actions.	HR professionals' jobs are not done if they simply speak with conviction. Their actions must lead to improvements, and it is necessary to gather data and evidence to corroborate or refute the efficacy of their actions. This step, again, should pertain for any business leader, but because HR has not been particularly data-driven in the past; it is an especially important step.
8. Becomes a role model for driving business results by: 1) Creating the context for talent and innovation to flourish, 2) Improving business results, and 3) Becoming a trusted and respected business leader.	The final quality of *The Fearless HR Mindset* is to pass it along by being a role model and teacher. This quality builds the legacy of HR Driving the Business, and helps to grow the profession both internally and externally. Given the various perceptions that have existed over the years, it takes time, focus and fertilization to build the *Fearless Mindset*.

Figure 9-3: Qualities of the Fearless HR Mindset

The term *Fearless* is a careful choice as the adjective for mindset and obviously the title of this book. Fearless has a strong and firm connotation, but it does not mean being reckless, arrogant, foolhardy or rushing to judgment. It is not an attitude, but a series of actions and qualities. A Fearless HR professional is one who is evidenced-based, sees the bigger picture, analyzes business issues, is a force-multiplier, and then, when ready to act, does so boldly and with a strong, resolute point of view. Every business leader must possess both deliberate and fearless qualities.

Tools and Templates

Tool 1: HR Perception Mindset Assessment

These perceptions, of course, are the ones treated in Part One of *Fearless HR*. This simple assessment may be useful for your team or colleagues as a means to discuss their views and perceptions of the current state of HR. Some very interesting conversations could ensue. It should be noted that the five perceptions are not independent of each other. If, for example, some believe that HR does not add value to the business, it is more than likely that they would also rate HR's tools and measures as being weak.

Perception of HR	Rating (Strongly agree =1 to Strongly disagree = 5)	Ranking (1 is most strongly held to 5 being least)	Comments
HR Doesn't Add Value to the Business			
HR is Siloed and Too Inwardly Focused			
HR is a Weak Discipline with Poor Tools			
HR Measures are Too Soft and Subjective			
HR is a Stodgy, Dead-end Career			

Tool 2: Marketing HR Purpose

It is often hard to see *Purpose* in organizations, but it shouldn't be. Organizations are a bundle of opportunities, but it is often up to HR to make these lines of sight to *Purpose* more explicit, first for ourselves and then for others. Once *Purpose* has been defined, then specific marketing campaigns should be identified and enacted. These campaigns may be simple communication efforts or more comprehensive multimedia campaigns with taglines for different audiences, but they are important. HR is typically very bad at marketing efforts, but the evidence is clear that a stronger link to *Purpose* improves engagement, which, in turn, raises customer satisfaction and financial returns.

Multiple Bottom Lines	Shared Purpose	Marketing Campaign
Business		
Workforce/Employees		
Community		
Society		

Tool 3: Multiple Bottom Lines and Purpose

Purpose is an accelerator of mindset, and HR's purpose—because it impacts the people of an organization who are, in turn, instrumental in creating value—is a distinct advantage compared to other groups or departments. Because organizations today are evaluated on multiple bottom lines (and not just profits), it is very meaningful to delineate all the ways in which HR can impact the business. From this list, each individual should pick those benefits (Owned Purpose) that are particularly meaningful to him or her.

Multiple Bottom Lines	**Purpose**	**Own Individual Purpose**
Business	Revenue growth Increased profits More new jobs Breakthrough products Products that improve lives High quality products Other:	
Workforce/ Employees	Flexible workplaces Offering developmental opportunities Providing new experiences Working with great colleagues Working together for shared purpose Growing professional networks Improving wellness and health Other:	
Community	Participation in the community Volunteerism Projects that improve conditions Other:	
Society	Improving the lives of citizens Green practices Preserving the environment Expanding opportunity Ethical principles Other:	

Tool 4: Fearless HR Meter

This tool is a simple pulse survey that can be used with HR peers and colleagues to track HR's perceived impact. It is different from Tool 1 which targets the general perceptions that people may hold of HR. There are two types of questions in this survey: ones that get to personal beliefs that HR professionals hold of themselves (1 through 4), and then views about the HR department/group as a whole (5 through 10). It may be interesting to see if responses differ by this grouping of items.

Pulse surveys are a good way to gather information quickly without overburdening employees.

Questions	Ratings	Comments
1. I believe that HR can drive business results		
2. I have the skills needed to be an effective business leader		
3. I use extensive data and evidence in making HR presentations to the leadership team		
4. My professional network is extensive and bridges different groups		
5. HR's contributions are respected by the management team		
6. HR has become a more respected force in the organization		
7. There are many examples of HR driving business results within the organization		
8. HR has talented employees who help the business succeed		
9. HR is viewed as a weak group within the organization		
10. HR doesn't provide much value to the organization		

Tool 5: *Fearless HR* Mindset Action Plan

This tool summarizes the treatment of the *Fearless HR* Mindset in this chapter. It provides a simple way to track progress on the key steps and qualities. It is important to remember that being Fearless is not just an attitude. It is whole series of activities that must occur for HR to drive business results.

Qualities of the Fearless HR Mindset	Actions Being Taken	Completion Date
Becomes Performance Ready.		
Understands HR Levers that Impact the Business.		
Believes in HR's Shared Purpose and Creates a Personal Owned Purpose.		
Analyzes Business Problems Using Data, a Systematic Approach and Communicates Effectively.		
Makes Compelling and Bold Business Cases.		
Is Accountable for Business Results.		
Seeks Evidence to Determine Effectiveness of Projects and Actions.		
Becomes a Role Model for Driving Business Results.		

Summary

Perhaps there is too much emphasis on strong new words for HR, such as fearless, bold, brave and even intrepid. But consider the history. The five historical perceptions of HR treated in Part One are not fabrications, and while some have historical justification, their relevance today should be challenged. It is clear that perceptions and biases can be changed, but not quickly or easily. It is also clear that perceptions linger, in spite of the evidence to the contrary. As I write these words, the latest issue of the Harvard Business Review is entitled: "It's Time to Blow Up HR and Build Something New…and Here's How." Really! Isn't this message several decades old?

Fearless HR is more about building HR to drive business results rather than buying, borrowing or blowing it up. Frameworks, models and tools have been presented that enable HR to drive business results, and not simply be an efficient internal function. HR can be a leader that drives the business, outdistances competitors and provides enduring value. This is the vision for HR moving forward, and to live this vision, HR must be fearless, bold and even courageous. But this does not mean simply exhibiting these attitudes, it means having the right skills and wisdom, constantly improving, knowing what impact can be achieved through HR Levers, having a conviction and strong point of view—backed by data and evidence, speaking truth to power if required, learning from past actions, and taking the necessary steps to ensure proper execution. When this is done, HR can:

- ☑ **Create the context in which talent and innovation can flourish**
- ☑ **Improve business results through better alignment to the triple bottom line, cost savings and productivity improvements**
- ☑ **Become a trusted and effective business leader**

CONCLUSION

One of the very best books I have read on people strategies driving business results--and creating contexts in which talent and innovation can flourish—comes from an unlikely source. It's an excellent source if you enjoy wonderful food; but it's an unlikely one for breakthrough practices that drive business results. Danny Meyer is one of the best-known restaurateurs in the world. His first flagship restaurants in New York City—Gramercy Tavern and the now closed Union Square Café—have provided legendary food and service for years. Other successful Danny Meyer restaurants have followed their example, and most recently their "hamburger joint" franchise, the Shake Shack, had a huge initial public offering. The secret to his success:

> *The only way a company can grow, stay true to its soul and remain consistently successful is to attract, hire and keep great people. It's that simple and it's that hard.....I continue to view people who work for me as volunteers.....I am convinced that a business cannot be more successful than the sum of the human relationships it has fostered and nurtured.*
>
> *Danny Meyer, Setting the Table, 2006*

A strong business focus provides clarity for the purpose and identity of HR. It is a laser focus, against which practices and initiatives can be aligned. It removes the clutter and distraction that has been imposed both by the HR profession itself and others. Before HR can embrace its business-driven future, it must confront the past perceptions that have dogged the profession over the years. When the evidence is examined, it is clear that there is nothing inherently wrong with the HR profession itself. There are too many examples of positive contributions and real impacts.

Despite countering past perceptions, a number of real hurdles exist before HR can drive the business forward. There are four key steps that must be taken. First, HR professionals must develop a greater diversity of skills and abilities. HR must "get better" and continually strive to improve in such a fast-changing world. Old skills and approaches will not suffice. Second, HR professionals need to expand and grow their professional networks as this becomes essential to developing capabilities and having access to the wisdom of others. Third, HR has very real levers to improve the business through better alignment, cost savings and productivity improvements. These levers need to be used in a balanced fashion, not simply through reductions in force or removing programs to save money. And fourth, the HR profession needs to speak with a new confidence, with perhaps even a bit of swagger. No other function touches all employees. No other function can truly be a force-multiplier.

The Fearless HR journey is now well known. It consists of overcoming past perceptions, before the new opportunities can be seized, so that the business results can be achieved.

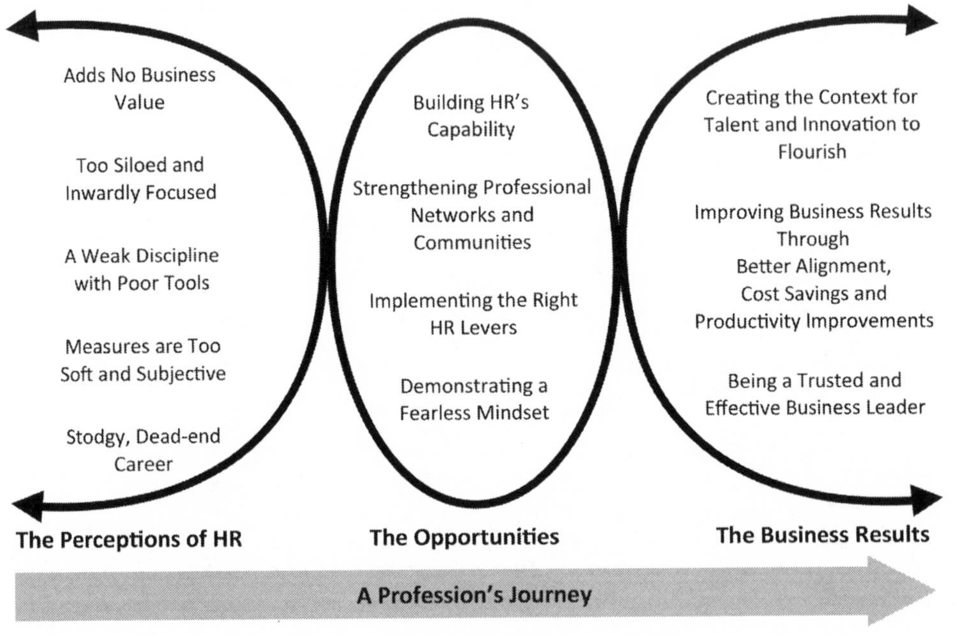

Excellence in engineering leads to strong products....
Excellence in finance leads to strong financial capabilities....
Excellence in HR leads to a great company.

Tony Parasida, Senior Vice President Human Resources and Administration, The Boeing Company

FIGURES

Tools

Fearless HR References and Readings

Anders, G. *The Rare Find: Spotting Exceptional Talent Before Everyone Else.* New York, NY: Portfolio/Penguin, 2011

Bassi, L. and McMurrer. "Maximizing Your Return on People." *Harvard Business Review.* March, 2007

Bassi, L., Frauenheim, E and McMurrer, D. *Good Company: Business Success in the Worthiness Era.* San Francisco, CA: Berret-Koehler, 2011

Bassi, L. *HR Analytics Handbook.* Amsterdam: Reed Business, 2012

Battilana, J. and Casciaro, T. "The Network Secrets of Great Change Agents." *Harvard Business Review.* July-August, 2013

Bauer, M. "Why Choose HR as a Career" *Demand Media.* 2015

Becker, B, Huselid, M and Ulrich, D. *The HR Scorecard.* Boston, MA: Harvard Business School Press, 2001

Becker, B, Huselid, M. and Beatty, R. *The Differentiated Workforce.* Boston, MA: Harvard Business School Press, 2009

Benko, C. and Weisberg, A. *Mass Career Customization.* Boston, MA: Harvard Business School Press, 2007

Benko, C. and Anderson, M. *The Corporate Lattice.* Boston, MA: Harvard Business School Press, 2010

Berger, L and Berger, D. *The Talent Management Handbook.* New York, NY: McGraw-Hill, 2011

Bergonzi, C. "Exploring the Neural Pathways pf Prejudice May Offer Clues to Lessening Its Effect." *Korn Ferry Briefings.* Issue 23

Berman, K. and Knight, J. *Financial Intelligence.* Boston, MA: Harvard Business Review Press, 2013

Bersin, J. "Predictions for 2014." Bersin by Deloitte, December, 2013

Bersin, J. "Predictions for 2015." Bersin by Deloitte. January, 2015

Bingham, T. and Conner, M. *The New Social Learning.* San Francisco, CA: Berret-Koehler, 2010

Boch, L. *Work Rules! Insights from Google that Will Transform How You Live and Lead.* New York, NY: Twelve, 2015

Breitfelder, D. and Dowling, D. "Why Did We Ever Go into HR?" *Harvard Business Review.* July- August, 2008

Burchell, M. and Robin, J. *The Great Workplace.* San Francisco, CA: Joeey-Bass, 2011

Bossidy, L. and Charan, R. Execution: *The Discipline f Getting Things Done.* New York: NY: Crown Business, 2002

Boudreau, J. and Ramstad, P. *Beyond HR: The New Science of Human Capital.* Boston, MA: Harvard Business School Press, 2007

Boudreau, J. *Retooling HR.* Boston, MA: Harvard Business Press, 2010

Boudreau, J. and Jesuthasan, R. *Transformative HR.* San Francisco, CA: Josey Bass, 2011

Boudreau, J. and Rice, S. "Bright, Shiny Objects and the Future of HR." *Harvard Business Review.* July-August, 2015

Branham, L. *The 7 Hidden Reasons Employees Leave.* New York, NY: AMACOM, 2005

Branson, R. *Screw Business as Usual.* New York, NY: Portfolio/Penguin, 2011

Briscoe, D., Schuler, R. and Claus, L. *International Human Resource Management.* London: UK. Routledge, 2009

Bryan, L and Joyce, C. *Mobilizing Minds.* New York, NY: McGraw-Hill, 2007

Buckingham, M. and Coffman, C. *First Break All the Rules.* New York, NY: Simon & Schuster, 1999

Buckingham, M. *The One Thing You Need to Know.* New York, NY: Simon & Schuster, 2005

Cacioppo, J. and Patrick, W. *Loneliness.* New York, NY: W.W. Norton & Company, 2009

Caligiuri, P., Lepak, D. and Bonache, J. *Managing the Global Workforce.* West Sussex, UK: John Wiley & Sons, 2011

Cantrell, S. and Smith, D. *The Workforce of One.* Boston, MA: Harvard Business Press, 2010

Cappelli, P. *Talent on Demand.* Boston, MA: Harvard Business Press, 2008

Capelli, P. Singh, H., Singh, J. and Useem, M. *The India Way.* Boston, MA: Harvard Business Press, 2010

Capelli, P. "Why We Love to Hate HR...and What HR Can Do About It." *Harvard Business Review.* July-August, 2015

Cascio, W. and Boudreau, J. *Investing in People*. Upper Saddle River, NJ: Pearson Education, 2008

Charan, R., Drotter, S. and Noel, J. *The Leadership Pipeline.* San Francisco, CA: Josey-Bass, 2001

Charan, R. *What the CEO Wants You to Know.* New York, NY: Crown Business, 2001

Charan, R. *Leaders at All Levels.* New York, NY: John Wiley, 2008

Charan, R. "It's Time to Split HR." *Harvard Business Review.* July-August, 2014

Charan, R., Barton, D. and Carey, D. "People Before Strategy: A New Role for the CHRO." *Harvard Business Review.* July-Augist, 2015

Collins, J. *Good to Great.* New York, NY: Harper Business, 2001

Collins, J. *How the Mighty Fall.* New York, NY: Harper Collins, 2009

Collins, J. and Hansen, M. *Great by Choice.* New York, NY: Harper Collins, 2011

Colvin, G. *Talent is Overrated: What really separates world-class performers from everybody else.* New York, NY: Penguin Group, 2008

Conant, D. and Norgaard, M. *TouchPoints.* San Francisco, CA: Jossey-Bass, 2011

Conaty, B. and Charan, R. *The Talent Masters.* New York, NY: Crown Business, 2010

Conley, C, *Peak.* San Francisco, CA: Jossey-Bass, 2007

Cope, K. *Seeing the Big Picture.* Austin, TX: Greenleaf Book Group, 2012

Covey, S. *The Speed of Trust.* New York, NY: Free Press, 2006

Cross, J. *Informal Learning.* San Francisco, CA: Pfieffer, 2007

Davenport, T.H. and Prusak, L. *Working Knowledge: How Organizations Manage What They Know*. Boston, MA: Harvard Business School Press, 2000

Davenport, T.H. and Harris, J. *Competing on Analytics: The New Science of Winning*. Boston, MA: Harvard Business School Press, 2007

Davenport, T.H, Harris, J. and Morison, R. *Analytics at Work.* Boston, MA: Harvard Business Press, 2010

Davenport, T.O, and Harding, S. *Manager Redefined.* San Francisco, CA: Jossey-Bass, 2010

Deloitte University Press. *Global Human Capital Trends 2014*

Deloitte University Press. *Global Human Capital Trends 2015*

Director, S. *Financial Analysis for HR Managers.* Saddle River, NJ: Pearson Education, 2013

Dweck, C. *Mindset.* New York, NY: Random House, 2006

Effron, M. and Ort, M. *One Page Talent Management.* Boston, MA: Harvard Business School Press, 2010

Evans, P., Pucik, V. and Bjorkman, I. *The Global Challenge.* New York, NY: McGraw-Hill, 2011

Filler, E. and Ulrich, D. "Why Chief Human Resource Officers Make Great CEOs." *Harvard Business Review.* December, 2014

Fishbein, M. "5 Best Types of People to Have in Your Network." Blog at mfishbein.com, 2015

Fitz-ens, J. *The ROI of Human Capital.* New York, NY: AMACOM, 2000 and 2009

Fleming, J. and Asplund, J. *Human Sigma.* New York, NY: Gallup Press, 2007

Florida, R. *The Flight of the Creative Class.* New York, NY: Harper Business, 2005

Forman, D. *The Principles of Human Capital Management.* Washington DC: Human Capital Institute, 2005

Forman, D. and Condit, R. "Compelling Business Cases." *HCI Conference Presentation,* 2011

Forman, D and Keene, B. "Revamping 70-20-10." *Chief Learning Officer.* October, 2012

Forman, D. "Stuck in Neutral." *Training and Development.* November, 2013

Forman, D. *The Decade of HR.* The Human Capital Institute, 2014

Forman, D. *"Analytics on Workforce Vulnerabilities"* Presentation at the Human Capital Institute Summit Conference, 2014

Friedman, T. *The World is Flat.* New York, NY: Farrat, Straus and Giroux, 2006

Friedman, T. and Mandelbaum, M. *That Used to be Us.* New York, NY: Farrar, Straus and Giroux, 2011

Friedman, T. "Hillary, Jeb, Facebook and Disorder." *New York Times.* May 20, 2015

Gardner, H. *Five Minds for the Future.* Boston, MA: Harvard Business School Press, 2006

Garvin, D. "How Google Sold Its Engineers on Management. *Harvard Business Review,* December, 2013

Gebauer, J. and Lowman, D. *Closing the Engagement Gap.* New York, NY: Portfolio Penguin, 2008

Gladwell, M. *Outliers.* New York, NY: Little Brown & Company, 2008

Godin, S. *Small is the New Big.* New York, NY: Penguin Group, 2006

Goffee, R. and Jones, G. "Creating the Best Workplace on Earth." *Harvard Business Review,* May, 2013

Govindarajan, V. and Trimble, C. *Reverse Innovation.* Boston, MA: Harvard Business Review Press, 2012

Hammonds, K. "Why We Hate HR." *Fast Company.* August, 2005

Hall, B. *The New Human Capital Strategy*. New York, NY: AMACOM, 2008

Hamel, G. *The Future of Management*. Boston, MA: The Harvard Business School Press, 2007

Hamel, G. *What Matters Now.* San Francisco, CA: Josey Bass, 2012

HBR Guide. *Finance Basics for Managers.* Boston, MA: Harvard Business Review Press, 2012

Harvard Business Review Analytic Services. "Taking Measure of Talent." Sponsored by Workday, 2014

Heath, C. and Heath, D. *Switch.* New York, NY: Broadway Books, 2010

Heskett, J, Sasser, E and Schlesinger, L. *The Service Profit Chain.* New York, NY: The Free Press, 1997

Heskett, J, Sasser, E. and Wheeler, J. *The Ownership Quotient.* Boston, MA: Harvard Business Review Press, 2008

Hoffman, R, Casnocha, B. and Yeh, C. *The Alliance.* Boston, MA: Harvard Business Review Press, 2014

Hsieh, T. *Delivering Happiness.* New York, NY: Business Plus, 2010

Human Capital Institute (HCI) Educational Courses: Human Capital Strategist; Strategic Workforce Planning; Building meaningful Analytics; and Strategic HR Business Partner, 2015

Human Capital Institute Research Studies with IBM and SAP, 2010

Huselid, M., Becker, B and Beatty, R. *The Workforce Scorecard.* Boston, MA: Harvard Business School Press, 2005

Hurst, A. *The Purpose Economy.* Boise, ID: Elevate, 2014

Kanter, R. *Supercorp.* New York, NY: Crown Business, 2009.

Kerr, S. *Reward Systems.* New York, NY: McGraw-Hill, 2009

Kotter, J. *Leading Change.* Boston, MA: Harvard Business School Press, 1996

Kotter, J. and Cohen, D, *The Heart of Change.* Boston, MA: Harvard Business School Press, 2002

Landel, M. "How Did We Do It: Sodexo's CEO on Smart Diversification." *Harvard Business Review,* March, 2015

Lawler, E. *Talent: Making People Your Competitive Advantage.* San Francisco, CA: Josey-Bass, 2008

Lawler, E, and Worley, C. *Management Reset.* San Francisco, CA: Josey-Bass, 2011

Lawler, E, and Boudreau, J. "Creating an Effective Human Capital Strategy." *HR Magazine,* August, 2012

Leonard, D. and Swapp, W. *Deep Smarts*. Boston, MA: Harvard Business School Press, 2005

Lev, B. *Intangibles.* The Brookings Institution Press, 2001

Meister, J and Willyerd, K. *The 2020 Workplace.* New York, NY: Harper Business, 2010

Meyer, D. *Setting the Table*. New York, NY: HarperCollins, 2006

Michaels, E., Handfield-Jones, H. and Axelrod, B. *The War for Talent.* Boston, MA: Harvard Business School Press, 2001

Murphy, M. *Hundred Percenters.* New York, NY: McGraw Hill, 2010

Murphy, M. *Hard Goals.* New York, NY: McGraw Hill, 2010

Myatt, M. "My Picks for the Top Ten CHROs and Why They Matter." *Forbes,* February, 2015

Nayar, V. *Employees First, Customers Second.* Boston, MA: Harvard Business Press, 2010

Nikravan, N. "Cisco: Divide and Conquer." *Talent Management.* February, 2014

Pease, G, Byerly, B. and Fitz-enz, J. *Human Capital Analytics.* New York, NY: John Wiley & Sons, 2013

Pfau, B. and Kay, I. *The Human Capital Edge.* New York, NY: McGraw Hill, 2002

Pfeffer, J. and Sutton, R. Hard Facts: *The Knowing-Doing Gap*. Boston, MA: Harvard Business School Press, 2000

Pfeffer, J. and Sutton, R. *Hard Facts: Profiting from Evidence-Based Management*. Boston, MA: Harvard Business School Press, 2006

Pink, D. *A Whole New Mind*. New York, NY: Riverhead Books, 2005

Pink, D. *Drive.* New York, NY: Riverhead Books, 2009

Pink, D. *To Sell is Human.* New York, NY: Riverhead Books, 2012

Polanyi, M. *Personal Knowledge.* Chicago, IL: University of Chicago Press, 1958

Rath, T. *Fully Charged.* Silicon Guild, 2015

PwCSaratoga. "Key Trends in Human Capital," 2012

Robertson, B. *Holacracy.* New York, NY: Henry Holt and Co, 2015

Rozin, P. and Royzman, E. "Negativity Bias, Negativity Dominance and Contagion." *Personality and Social Psychology Review,* 2001

Rumelt, R. *Good Strategy/Bad Strategy.* New York: NY: Crown Business, 2011

Sartain, L. and Schuman, M. *Brand From The Inside.* San Francisco, CA: Jossey-Bass, 2006

Schiemann, W. *Reinventing Talent Management.* Hoboken, NJ: John Wiley & Sons, 2009

Scullion, H. and Collins, D. *Global Talent Management.* New York, NY: Routledge, 2011

Seidman, D. *How.* Hoboken, NJ: John Wiley & Sons, 2007

Semler, R. *The Seven-Day Weekend.* London, UK: Century, 2003

Slap, S. *Bury My Heart at Conference Room B.* New York, NY: Portfolio Penguin, 2010

Society for Human Resource Management (SHRM). "SHRM Body of Knowledge and Competency." 2015

Smith, K. "It's Time for Companies to Fire Their Human Resource Departments." *Forbes.* April, 2013

Sutton, R. and Rao, H. *Scaling Up Excellence.* New York, NY: Crown Business, 2014

Su, A. and Wilkins, M. *Own the Room.* Boston, MA: Havard Business Review Press, 2013

Taylor, W. and LaBarre, P. *Mavericks at Work.* New York, NY: William Morrow, 2006

Ulrich, D. and Brockbank, W. *The HR Value Proposition*. Boston, MA: Harvard Business School Press, 2005

Ulrich, N. and Smallwood, N. *Why the Bottom Line Isn't.* New York, NY: John Wiley, 2003

Ulrich, D., et. al. *HR Competencies*. Washington DC: Society for Human Resource Management, 2008

Ulrich, D, et. al. *The Leadership Code.* Boston, MA: Harvard Business Press, 2008

Ulrich, D and Ulrich, W. *The Why of Work.* New York, NY: McGraw Hill, 2010

Ulrich, D, Younger, J, Brockbank, W and Ulrich, M. *HR from the Outside In.* New York, NY: McGraw Hill, 2012

Wagner, R. and Harter, J. *12: The Elements of Great Managing.* New York, NY: Gallup Press, 2006

Watkins, M. *The First 90 Days*. Boston, MA: Harvard Business School Press, 2003

Welch, J. *Winning.* New York, NY: Harper Business, 2005

Weatherly, L. "Human Capital—The Elusive Asset." *Society for Human Resource Management,* 2003

Wiseman, L. *Multipliers.* New York, NY: Harpers Business, 2010.

Zenger, J and Folkman, J. *The Extraordinary Leader.* New York, NY: McGraw Hill, 2002

Zenger, J., Folkman, J and Edinger, S. *The Inspiring Leader.* New York, NY: McGraw Hill, 2009

ACKNOWLEDGEMENTS

I hope you will indulge me, because I have a lot of thanks to give. This book is really a culmination of, not just the 15 years of my direct involvement with HR, but my whole career. I encourage a quick skimming for most of you, but for the people who have been so helpful to me, I want to say thank you publically. The best way to do this is to briefly recount the stops that Linda and I have made over the years. It begins quite a while ago.

- ***Murray Thomas and the University of California at Santa Barbara (UCSB).*** Linda and I met at UCSB as undergraduates, and after four years in the Air Force, I returned to graduate school. Linda worked to support our young family, while I attempted to get smarter. My graduate advisor in international education was Murray Thomas, and Murray has been my teacher, role model and friend for forty years. We e-mailed just last week, and he is enjoying his 94th birthday (Summer 2015). He is one of the most remarkable people I have ever met. After retiring from the UCSB faculty, he has kept somewhat busy by writing 18 books (after retiring!), completing books of verse and creating beautiful watercolors. It's Churchillian in variety and breadth of accomplishment.

  But Murray's lessons for me happened far earlier. As an uncertain graduate student, he guided me around corners, showed compassion and toughness, and helped me meld adult learning theory, research design, measurement and evaluation, systems thinking and the skill of synthesizing different perspectives together into a skill set I use to this day. Murray also taught me about the nobleness of being a teacher. It is, he said, the finest of professions. May you all have a Murray Thomas in your life.

- ***Lincoln Nebraska and Teheran, Iran (1973-1977).*** My first real job after graduate school was at the University in Mid-America in Lincoln, Nebraska. As an evaluator and instructional designer in a federally funded project, I came to know bright young professionals with newly minted doctorates from Stanford, Syracuse, and Illinois. We all learned together, equally from our mistakes and successes. From these early connections, a whole host of opportunities opened up, not the least of which was work at Children's Television Workshop and overseas in Iran in 1977. Thank you to Dennis Gooler, John Eggert, Fran Aversa, Beau Vallance, Roger Sell and Penny Richardson.

Our little family spent an amazing year in Iran in 1977 in a graduate program affiliated with Syracuse University. I taught research and evaluation to about 20 students who were developing radio and television programs to be broadcast to rural schools in Iran. Linda taught English as a second language to the students who required further assistance. People thought we were nuts to take this year, but it was truly one of the great experiences of our lives. Great people, amazing country, and the richest of experiences to travel and live in another culture. Thank you John Eggert (again), David Chapman, Carol Williamson and Bill and Susan Prescott.

- ***Boston, Spectrum Interactive and NETg (1981-1995).*** Boston was our home for 15 years, and where our boys grew up. I joined a small training company founded by George Haskell and Karen Lawrence, and it morphed into a number of different companies and owners. I was given more responsibility than I probably deserved, but the major account experience proved priceless, whether creating multimillion dollar projects for Ford, Target and Federal Express; introducing the Macintosh with Apple, implementing major reskilling efforts with IBM or working with the Harvard Business School on embedded simulations. Ines Machado was a great colleague each step along the way.

  Eventually I became President of Spectrum Interactive and part of the senior management team of National Education Training Group (NETg). My business focus was greatly developed during these years. There are so many people who helped forge me during these fifteen years, thank you to one and all. I do want to single out John Kirkham who headed the global business for NETg. John goes way back to ASI, Deltak, and Applied Learning days. He has forgotten more about the training business than most people know, and he was gracious in helping me learn the ropes. Thankfully, I was able to repay him on the tennis court on occasion.

- ***St Louis and Wave Technologies (1995-1999).*** In 1995, we moved to St Louis to once again work with John Kirkham and a talented team in the IT training market. Here I created new products, simulation engines and multimedia games with Curt Todd, Deb Smith, Scott Fillenworth, Frank Miller and Rachelle Reese. It is here at Wave that I rediscovered the pleasure I got from creating new products and getting back to "doing the work," as opposed to managing people who manage people. This led to moving to San Diego, opening up Sage Learning Systems and my involvement with HR.

- ***SHRM and the Global Learning System (2002).*** We moved to San Diego to be closer to Linda's mother and to open Sage Learning Systems so that we could get back to creating and developing solutions ourselves. One of the first big contracts Sage won was to develop the first Global HR learning system in support of SHRM's new GPHR certification. It included six books, CD-ROM, e-learning modules, gaming and simulations. The project lasted more than a year, and I worked with an amazing group of HR experts from all over the world who contributed both to the materials and my own development. Thank you to Lisbeth Claus, Steve Miranda, Carolyn Gould, John Eggert and SHRM's beloved David C Forman—my exact namesake (although we had never met) who has since passed.

- ***The Human Capital Institute (2004-2015).*** My time with HCI started innocently enough with a discussion with founder Mike Foster on creating a course or two on leveraging the human capital of organizations. In 2004, there were not many models to follow. So I created a few, and a decade later more than 10,000 people worldwide have taken these courses and now carry HCI certifications. I experienced, first hand, what Murray Thomas meant about the finest profession. I really enjoyed my time with students in the classroom and subsequently as host of HCI conferences. *Fearless HR* came from many of these encounters, questions and conversations.

Again, there have been so many people to thank for building what we built. It is a tribute to all of you. My shout outs go to Mike Foster for his vision, Nigel Leeming for his business sense and judgment—especially in the precarious early years, Bill Craib for his direction and support, the sales team who make it happen every day—pros like Shane Lennon, and Frank McLaughlin; the HCI Faculty including long-time members Mark Allen, Bruce Walton and Glen Kallas, and all of the educational operations team over the years from Barbara to Kate to Melissa to Krystin. You're the best. I wish good fortune to the current management team of Carl, Angela, Shane, Barry, Katie and Kara.

I would also like to acknowledge one corporate HCI client out of many. The Boeing Company has made a three year commitment to improve the capabilities of its HR professionals. The vehicle is called the Capstone program and is comprised mainly of HCI materials. Boeing's core team of Bryan Hunt, Gary Walters, Sara Gibbs and Jed Sawyer have been exceptional from the start. And Boeing's HR leaders including Tony Parasida and Norma Clayton have not only supported Capstone from the outset, they have been to most sessions and made major contributions. I am indebted to the entire Boeing team and Capstone participants for their support and contributions to *Fearless HR*.

- ***The Fearless HR Team.*** While it is probably now painfully obvious that many people have influenced my thinking and development over the years, and therefore the messages in *Fearless HR*. There are a handful of us most directly responsible for this book. I am solely responsible for the content coverage, validity and interpretations. I have taken great care to be true to the works of others. If I have inadvertently misrepresented them in any way, please let me know and I apologize.

Linda Forman has read every page and has been enormously helpful from an editing, flow and continuity perspective. Her suggestions have materially improved the book in so many ways. Bruce Walton, an HCI faculty member and lifelong friend from days in Boston, leads a team of content reviewers, including Sean Nelson, Mark Berry, and HCI faculty members, to challenge me and sharpen the key messages. Parissa Esmaili takes my drafts and turns them into a finished product. She is patient, thoughtful and artistic, and these are all great qualities to bring to the team. And a special thanks to Dave Ulrich for writing such a meaningful and insightful Foreword. Thank you all.

Close Friends and Family. This is the hard part. None of us can do what we do without loved ones being close. And eloquent writers have expressed thanks to these special people far more beautifully than I ever could. But this doesn't mean that I should remain silent.

First, while Linda and I have lived all across the country having many different experiences, we have always reconnected with Ron and Erica Rubenstein. Ron was my college roommate, has gotten us involved again with the UCSB board, is a tough competitor on the tennis court and has somewhat unique eating habits; but both Ron and Erica have been great and valued friends.

Our San Diego family is Linda's sister Annie, and her daughter Tiffany's family: husband Barry, sons Ben and Jake plus dogs. I had the wonderful honor of giving Tiffany away at her wedding, and will always treasure this experience. Thank you guys for giving us family so close.

Our boys, Christian and Andrew, live on the East Coast with their beautiful families. Chris is the founder and CEO of two innovative companies in the talent acquisition arena. He does all this while living on an 1830s New England farm with cows, pigs, sheep, and a covered bridge next door. Chris is married to his Colby sweetheart, Dr. Angela Toms, and they have four wonderful children: Emma, Noah, Will and Sara. Andy is a partner in a leading global law firm, aspiring writer, devoted Red Sox and Patriots fan, husband to Amy and father to Jamie and Max. Amy is the head of a terrific pre-school program in Bethesda, Maryland. And to Ariel, who lived with us in high school through the ABC program, and has been along with Sarah, Ari and Juliana, part of our family ever since. The fact that our kids are now amazing parents themselves is one of life's great joys.

Two other people who remain with me even though they are not here. My mother—Eileen Halligan Forman—educated at Smith College, friend to Julia Child, lover of literature and art, kept the family together while my father was caught in the transition from being an actor in radio to a television personality. Mom enabled Gail, Judy and me to grow up in a loving environment, took a job as a school secretary to support the family, and always demonstrated grace and class, even in difficult times.

Linda's father—Joseph Jameson McCandless—grew up in Northern Ireland, never graduated from high school, came to the US in the 1920s, drove a horse-drawn laundry cart in Los Angeles, sent an engagement ring in the mail back to Ireland to Margaret Bingham—who then set sail across the Atlantic to marry him after never being more than 15 miles from her home. Joe, who loved the land and living things, founded Rockview Milk Farms, grew it into the largest independent dairy in Southern California, and had an unquenchable curiosity and energy that would always lead to new products and business ideas years ahead of anyone else. Talk about driving business results and blue ocean strategies. Joe was a father to all of us.

The last and most important acknowledgement is for Linda. All that I can say is that I simply could not do without you. It just wouldn't work, and it wouldn't be any fun. So thank you for every day and all that you are. On to our next 50.

> *I am a lucky man, to count on many hands, the people that I love*
>
> *Pearl Jam*

Index

INDEX

A

B

C

D

E

F

G

H

I

J

K

L

M

N

O

P

Q

R

S

T

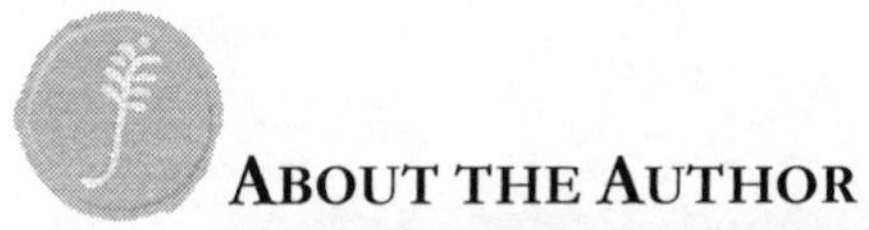

About the Author

David C Forman is the President of Sage Learning Systems and former Chief Learning Officer of The Human Capital Institute. The courses he has developed and taught for HCI have been taken by thousands of HR professionals all over the world. In 2002, David worked with SHRM to create materials to support the GPHR certification program. Prior to these experiences, David spent 25 years in the training industry, working with large global organizations to improve the knowledge, skills and performance of their people. Major clients include FedEx, IBM, DuPont, Microsoft, SAP, American Express, PwC, Ford, Prudential, Apple, Scripps Healthcare, Allstate Insurance and the University of Farmers. In 1984, David had the unique opportunity to work with Apple on the release of the Macintosh; and several years later to help IBM streamline and cross-train over 22,000 manufacturing employees.

David has written more than 40 articles on talent management, analytics, strategic human resources, learning systems, high-performance cultures and leadership. He has also spoken at many national and global talent and leadership conferences, both in his role of hosting HCI's conferences for many years but also as a keynote speaker.

After living in such diverse places as Santa Barbara, Nebraska, Boston, St Louis and Teheran, Iran; David and Linda now reside in San Diego, California. Their sons live on the East Coast with their families.